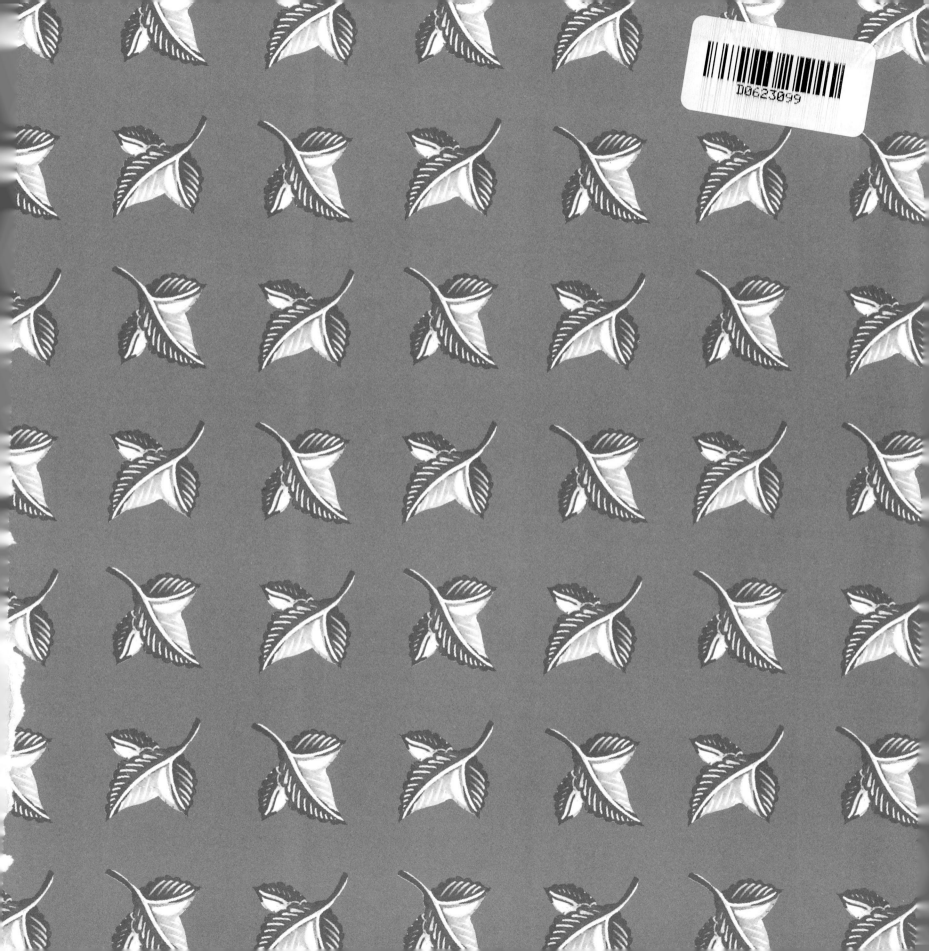

perfect
small gardens

perfect
small gardens

Peter McHoy, Barbara Segall
and Stephanie Donaldson

LORENZ BOOKS

This edition published by Lorenz Books in 2002

© Anness Publishing Limited 1997, 2002

Lorenz Books is an imprint of Anness Publishing Limited
Hermes House, 88–89 Blackfriars Road, London SE1 8HA

Published in the USA by Lorenz Books, Anness Publishing Inc.
27 West 20th Street, New York, NY 10011

www.lorenzbooks.com

This edition distributed in Canada by Raincoast Books
9050 Shaughnessy Street, Vancouver, British Columbia V6P 6E5

A CIP catalogue record for this book is available from the British Library.

Publisher: Joanna Lorenz
Project Editors: Lindsay Porter & Helen Sudell
Designers: Peter Laws, Lilian Lindblom, Alan Marshall & David Stanley
Photographer: John Freeman
Illustrator: Michael Shoebridge

Previously published as *Practical Small Gardens*

1 3 5 7 9 10 8 6 4 2

CONTENTS

Introduction	**6**
DESIGNING THE GARDEN	**8**
CREATING THE GARDEN STRUCTURE	**42**
CREATING PLANTING SCHEMES	**78**
CONTAINER GARDENING	**126**
GARDENING PRACTICALITIES	**156**
THE GOOD PLANT GUIDE	**178**
Index	**189**
Acknowledgements	**192**

INTRODUCTION

Gardening is something more than a collection of plants in beds and borders – it is about creating an overall effect, a statement of your idea of a good garden in which the plants and the hard landscaping (paving and walls, for example) both play a vital part. This book shows you how to stamp your own identity on every aspect of your garden, from the planning stage to your choice of containers, whatever the limitations of time and space.

The importance of comprehensive planning is stressed in the opening section, *Designing the Garden.* With its design ideas for even the most unpromising plots, this section will enable you to make the most of the specific advice offered later in the book. In the two main sections of the book, *Creating the Garden Structure* and *Creating Planting Schemes*, all sorts of wonderful suggestions are made: some conventional (lawns and formal borders), some less so (water features and the "wild" look).

Containers, thanks to their mobility and versatility, can also play a significant role in shaping the overall look of a garden, and, in *Container Gardening*, there are many suggestions for beautiful plantings for every season of the gardening year. What most gardeners wish to avoid is spending excessive amounts of time on the more mundane tasks such as feeding and weeding. *Gardening Practicalities* demonstrates how to tackle the essential jobs effectively and with the minimum of fuss. Finally, *The Good Plant Guide* provides a handy reference as you plan your planting schemes.

Designing the Garden

Thorough and realistic planning is the key to successful gardening. Whether you are starting from scratch or redesigning an existing plot it is vital to have in mind an overall scheme and a set of priorities before you begin to erect your fence or plant your border. Even if your garden is awkward in shape or situation, you can create the environment you want, provided you follow a few simple principles of design.

Left: *A small garden should not lack impact. Provided it is well planted and has some strong focal points, it becomes easy to ignore the limitations of size.*

Above: *A sense of mystery and excitement can be created simply by adding ornaments and providing a hidden area of the garden to be explored.*

Principles of Design

With a few exceptions – such as wild gardens or those with an informal country cottage style, for example – the hallmark of a well-designed garden is that it has either a strong theme or detectable pattern. If your interest lies primarily in plants, then clever planting patterns, or pretty color themes, or contrast will be enough to give your garden that special look. Usually, however, it is the hard landscaping that gives a garden a strong sense of having been designed.

One way to guarantee impact in a small area is to mix paving materials and introduce small changes in level.

The design here has a strongly rectangular theme, but because of the variety of textures and changes of level, it doesn't look boring.

This professionally designed garden also shows the importance of foliage plants and the role of moving water as a focal point.

This combination of both a creative use of plants and strong hard landscaping has the indisputable hallmark of careful planning and design. Even in a small area like this, the impact is immediate.

Circular themes can be difficult to accommodate in a small garden, and where the circles leave awkward angles, they can be hard to manage. Here the problem has been overcome by the clever use of water, with bold plants to help mask transition points.

The choice of a single specimen plant with an almost spherical outline, off-set to one side of the decking, combines simplicity with good taste and a strong sense of design. Garden size is less important than how you use the space.

As a basic shape, gardens cannot be any simpler than this, but even a quick glance tells you that it has the stamp of a very experienced designer. The plants in this country garden have that magical cottage garden look, yet they have been framed in a clearly modern setting.

Bricks and clay pavers are an excellent choice for this kind of informal planting as they have a mellowness that complements the plants. This very simple design works so well because the pavers have been laid in an interesting herringbone pattern with a crisp outline around the inner bed.

Focal points are very important, and even a potentially dull or boring corner of the garden can be transformed into an area of special charm with the imaginative use of a focal point. Before a focal point was introduced, this small path led between some shrubs to the boundary hedge, and was a serviceable part of the garden that you would not want to show your visitors. A couple of slate steps and a Japanese lantern set in a small graveled area were all that was needed to transform this area into a feature that seldom fails to attract favorable comment.

Improving your garden does not necessarily mean a major redesign. Often, only small changes or the clever use of focal points are all that is required.

Left: *Multiple and linking circles always make a better design than individual or isolated circular areas. This design is particularly effective because the circular pond is reflected in the edging, the band of grass, and then the surrounding brick path, rather like ripples in a pool. By using the same bricks for the path leading to this part of the garden, the whole feature has been well integrated.*

Above: *If you take over a mature garden, with large trees and shrubs, you may feel that major reconstruction would be too demanding. Often, however, a few simple modifications will achieve a transformation.*

The addition of a couple of formal beds edged with box is sufficient to transform a plain lawn into something more formal that seems appropriate for this style of older garden. But it still needs color and a central focal point to create a sense of design, and here it has been achieved with a large and attractively planted urn.

To give your garden a strong appeal, it is not necessary to destroy most of what is there already. Sometimes it is sufficient to remove one or two features and perhaps create an area of strong visual appeal in their place.

Deciding on Priorities

It makes sense to begin any garden design by making a wish-list. It is most unlikely to be fulfilled completely, but setting down those things that are a priority to you should insure that the most important features are included.

MAKING YOUR LIST

Everyone has different preferences, so make a list like the one shown here (photocopy it if you don't want to write your own or mark the book). Decide which features you regard as essential (this may be something as mundane as a clothes-dryer or as interesting as a water feature), those that are important but less essential for your ideal garden, and those elements that you regard simply as desirable. While designing your garden, keep in mind those features listed as essential. Try to incorporate as many of them as possible, but don't cram in so many that the strong sense of design is sacrificed.

It will immediately become apparent if the list of the most desirable features is not feasible within the limited space available, but you will probably be able to introduce some of the more important ones. However, only attempt to include those features checked as desirable if you have space.

Working from a check-list will not directly aid the design, but it will act as a reminder of what is important to you. A garden that fulfils the functions that are important may be more satisfying than one that is well designed and smart but omits features that you care about.

GARDEN PRIORITIES

	Essential	Important	Desirable
Flowerbeds	[ ]	[ ]	[ ]
Perennial border	[ ]	[ ]	[ ]
Shrub border	[ ]	[ ]	[ ]
Trees	[ ]	[ ]	[ ]
Lawn	[ ]	[ ]	[ ]
Graveled area	[ ]	[ ]	[ ]
Paved area/patio	[ ]	[ ]	[ ]
Built-in barbecue	[ ]	[ ]	[ ]
Garden seats/furniture	[ ]	[ ]	[ ]
Rock garden	[ ]	[ ]	[ ]
Pond	[ ]	[ ]	[ ]
Other water feature	[ ]	[ ]	[ ]
Wildlife area	[ ]	[ ]	[ ]
Greenhouse/ conservatory	[ ]	[ ]	[ ]
Summerhouse	[ ]	[ ]	[ ]
Toolhouse	[ ]	[ ]	[ ]
Fruit garden	[ ]	[ ]	[ ]
Herb garden	[ ]	[ ]	[ ]
Vegetable garden	[ ]	[ ]	[ ]
Trellis/ arbor/arch	[ ]	[ ]	[ ]
Sandpile play area	[ ]	[ ]	[ ]
Clothes-dryer	[ ]	[ ]	[ ]
Compost pile	[ ]	[ ]	[ ]
Recycling bins	[ ]	[ ]	[ ]
Trash cans	[ ]	[ ]	[ ]
....	[ ]	[ ]	[ ]
....	[ ]	[ ]	[ ]
	[ ]	[ ]	[ ]

Be flexible in your approach to features. If a pond is on your list but there does not seem to be sufficient space or an appropriate place to build it, consider a small patio pond like this one.

The toolhouse is always difficult to accommodate, as it should not be obtrusive. With clever planting, however, it can usually be screened well enough to be acceptable.

A permanent barbecue may look impressive when entertaining, but bear in mind that it can also look bleak in winter. You may prefer a portable one that can be removed when it is not required.

Right: *If you want an arbor but there is not space for a free-standing one, an alternative is a patio that links house and garden. Linking house and garden visually is important in good garden design.*

Surveying and Measuring

It is much better – and less expensive – to make your mistakes on paper first, so the starting point for any garden improvement plan should be to prepare a pencil sketch and plan of the garden as it is. This can then be worked up into any number of imaginative designs, and if things do not work out as you expected, just erase it or put it in the recycling bin, and start again.

WHAT YOU WILL NEED

- A 100-foot tape measure – preferably plasticized fabric as this is easy to work with, but does not stretch.
- A 6-foot steel rule for short measurements.
- Pegs to mark out positions, and to hold one end of the tape in position (meat skewers can be used with the tape).
- Pencils, sharpener and eraser.
- Clipboard with pad or graph paper.

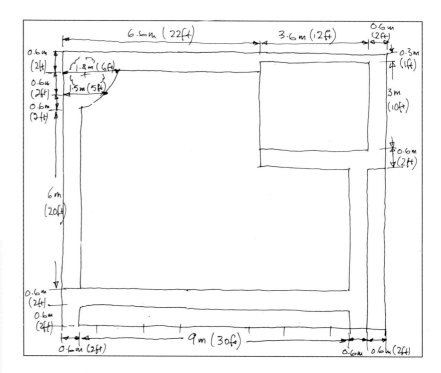

Make a rough freehand sketch of the garden. If it is very large, divide it into sections that can be pieced together later, but for a small garden like this, the whole area will go onto a single sheet of paper.

If necessary, join several sheets of paper together rather than cramp the sketch, and leave plenty of space around the edge on which you can write the dimensions.

Write down the measurements of all the main features, like paths, sheds and greenhouses, and important flowerbeds and large trees. Do not include anything that you are already sure you will not retain, otherwise include as many measurements as possible.

COPING WITH SLOPES

- Professional landscape architects surveying a large garden will use special techniques to determine the slope, which is then transferred to the plan as contour lines. However, most simple garden improvements can be achieved quite successfully without this degree of accuracy.

- If the slope is very gradual, you can ignore it, unless you want to create a deliberate change of level. More significant slopes can usually be estimated and the contours drawn in by eye. If the slope is steep, or if you want to create a series of terraces, you will have to measure the slope accurately and incorporate it into your scale drawing. Usually, however, it is possible to improve your garden simply by using the methods suggested in this book.

POSITIONING FEATURES

With a small rectangular garden, like the one shown here, most measurements are easily determined by measuring key points from a known straight line such as the house or a fence. If the shape is more complicated, it is usually possible to determine a position by laying a piece of string at right angles from the known straight edge, then measuring at right angles from this at a point marked on your sketch. This avoids the slightly more complicated method of positioning such as triangulation, described on page 17.

Gentle slopes over a short distance seldom present a problem. A couple of very shallow terraces that do not need strong retaining walls are usually sufficient to create plenty of level ground for a lawn, for example, and then the final steeper bank can be clothed with rock plants. These will look attractive, tolerate the dry conditions found on sloping ground and, once established, will help to stabilize the soil.

Putting the Plan on Paper

The exciting part of replanning your garden starts when you have an outline of the existing garden and permanent fixtures on which you can start to create your dream garden. It has all the excitement and promise of reading seed catalogs, where the imagination transforms the existing garden into an area full of beauty and promise. Making an accurate scale drawing of your existing garden is an essential starting point if you want to simplify the design work that follows.

QUICK ON THE DRAW

1 Draw the outline of the garden first, together with the position of the house and any other features, and make sure you have the correct measurements for these before filling in the other elements.

2 Next, draw in those elements that are easy to position, such as rectangular flowerbeds or raised beds and the toolhouse, if you are reasonably certain of exactly where they are.

3 Ink in those elements of the garden that are fixed and will not change, such as boundaries and paths that you know you will not move. Draw the other parts in pencil first, as it is quite likely that you may have to make slight adjustments. Ink them in when you know everything is in its correct place.

4 Use a compass if possible to draw curves and circles. Not all curves are suitable for this treatment, but you can buy flexible rules that can be bent to any reasonable curve.

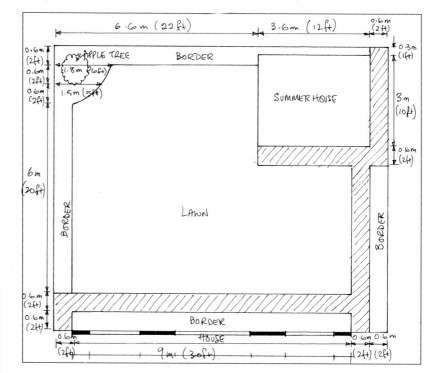

The rough sketch must be transferred to a scale drawing before any detailed plans can be sketched out. Drawing it to scale will help you in calculating the amount of any paving required, and also enable you to make beds, borders and lawns to sizes that involve the least amount of cutting of hard materials such as paving slabs or bricks.

Use graph paper for your scale drawing. Pads are adequate for a small garden or a section of a larger one, but if your garden is big, buy a large sheet (available from good stationers and art supply stores).

Use a scale that enables you to fit the plan onto your sheet of graph paper (or several taped together). For most small gardens, a scale of 1:50 (¼ inch to 1 foot) is about right. For a large garden, however, 1:100 (⅛ inch to 1 foot) might be more appropriate.

Draw the basic outline and the position of the house first, including the position of doors and windows if relevant. Then add all the major features that you are likely to retain. You should have all the necessary measurements on the freehand sketch that you made in the garden.

Omit any features that you are sure will be eliminated from the new design, to keep it as uncluttered as possible. In this example, the summerhouse has been drawn in because it was considered to be in a good position and would be difficult to move. The corner tree was removed in the final design, but was included at this stage as a design might have been chosen that made use of it.

USING YOUR PLAN

1 Even expert designers make a number of rough sketches of possible designs before finalizing the chosen one, so devise a way of using your master outline again and again without having to keep redrawing it. One way is to make a number of photocopies.

2 If you have a drawing board, simply use tracing paper overlays for your roughs while experimenting with ideas. If you do not have a drawing board and the garden is small, you may be able to use a clipboard instead.

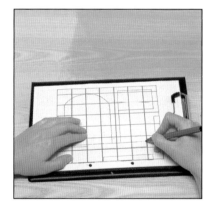

3 Film and pens of the type used for overhead projection sheets are effective if you prefer to use colors that can be wiped off easily for correction.

4 Some people prefer visual aids to move around when designing. If you find this helpful, try drawing and cutting out scale features that you want to include in your finished design, such as a raised pond, patio furniture, or raised beds. These can be moved around until they look right, but they should only be used as aids once the overall design has been formulated in your mind. If you try to design your garden around the few key symbols that you have placed, it will lack. coherence.

DESIGNING BY COMPUTER

- If you feel happier with a computer keyboard and mouse than with paper and pencil, you can use one of the several computer programs that are available to help you design your garden.

- These vary enormously in capability and ease of use. The cheaper ones are likely to be fairly basic, and you may find them more frustrating to use than you imagine. The more sophisticated programs are both versatile and effective, but unless you intend to design gardens on a regular basis, they are probably not worth the money and time needed to learn how to use them properly.

- You will find pencil and paper just as effective for a working design for your own garden, with minimal financial outlay and the decided advantage of being able to move around your garden while modifying the plan (unless of course you want to do it all on a portable computer).

TRIANGULATION MADE EASY

- Sometimes it may be difficult to measure a position simply by using right angles: perhaps there is an obstruction such as a pond or low hedge, for example, or there may be no available right angles because of the shape of the garden. Triangulation is a way of fixing a position, and is much easier than it sounds.

- Using known points, the corners of the house in this example, simply measure the distance to the position to be fixed, and note the two distances on your sketch.

- When you make your scale drawing, set a compass to each of the scale distances in turn, then strike an arc in the approximate position. The point you measured in the garden is where the arcs intersect on the plan.

To fix the position of the tree, measure to A, then B. Strike arcs on a scale drawing with compasses set at these measurements. The point where the arcs cross indicates the position of the tree in relation to the house.

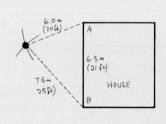

Creating your Design

The difficult part of redesigning or improving your garden is making a start. After you start drawing, the ideas are sure to flow, especially if you have other gardens in mind that you like and can use as a starting point. The many inspirational pictures in this book will provide a wealth of ideas that you can adapt for your own garden, but take elements from various gardens that you like rather than try to recreate someone else's design exactly. Designs seldom transfer easily unless your garden is very similar in shape and size, and your garden will be much more satisfying if it reflects your own personality and preferences.

PLANNING THE SHAPE OF THE GARDEN

If you decide on a garden with strong lines, rather than irregular flowing borders, wildlife corners and semi-woodland areas, it is worth deciding on whether you are going to plan a rectangular or diagonal theme, or use a design based on circles. Any of these can be adapted to suit the size of your garden, and in the case of the circular pattern, you might want to include overlapping circles. Where circles join, try to make any transitional curves gradual rather than abrupt.

Whichever you choose, draw a grid on top of your plan to aid design (see opposite page). In a small garden surrounded by fencing, it can be useful to base the rectangular and diagonal grids on the spacing of fence posts (usually about 6 feet apart).

A rectangular grid has been used for the example opposite, but as part of the trial-and-error phase, it is usually worth trying different grids. A diagonal grid is often particularly effective where the house is set in a large garden with plenty of space at the sides. The patio can often be positioned at a 45-degree angle at the corner of the house, for example.

The size and shape of the garden will usually dictate the most appropriate grid, but if in doubt, try more than one to see which one emerges with more possibilities than the others after a few attempts at quick designs.

Bear in mind that many excellent, prize-winning gardens are created without such a grid, and sometimes these have, to some extent, evolved in a more flowing manner, developing feature by feature. Grids like these may help you, but do not hesitate to adopt a more freestyle approach if this comes more naturally.

CIRCULAR THEME

DIAGONAL THEME

RECTANGULAR THEME

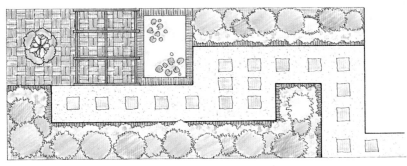

BEGINNING THE DESIGN

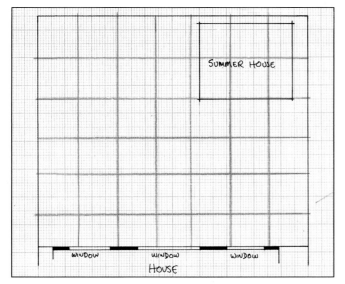

1 Draw in any features to be retained (in this example the summerhouse), and the chosen grid (unless you want an informal style where a grid may be inappropriate). Use a different color for the grid lines, in order to prevent the plan becoming cluttered and confused.

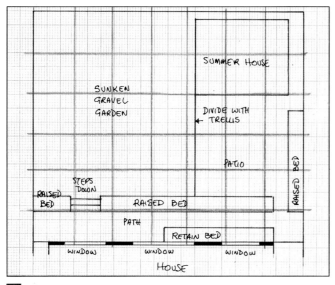

2 Use overlays (or photocopies) to experiment with a range of designs. Even if the first attempt looks satisfactory, try a number of variations. You can always come back to your first idea later if it turns out to be the best one.

At this stage, do not include details such as patio furniture or individual plants (except for key focal point plants and important trees or shrubs). When you have a design that you like, pencil in things like patio furniture (or use the cut-out features if you prepared them earlier).

TEN TIPS TO TRY

Don't despair if inspiration does not come easily, or initial attempts seem disappointing. If you try these ten tips, you will almost certainly produce workable plans that you will be pleased with:

• Look through books and magazines to decide which style of garden you like: formal or informal; the emphasis on plants or on hard landscaping; mainly foliage, texture and ground cover or lots of colorful flowers; straight edges or curved and flowing lines.

• With the style decided, look at as many garden pictures as possible – make a start in this book – and look for design ideas that appeal. Do not be influenced by individual plants, as these can be changed.

• Choose a grid, if applicable, as described on page 18, and draw this onto your plan. This will help to carry your thoughts through on logical lines.

• Start sketching lots of designs but do not attempt to perfect them at this stage. Just explore ideas.

• Do not concern yourself with planning plants or attempt to choose individual plants at this stage – concentrate on patterns and lines.

• Do not spend time drawing in paving patterns or choosing materials yet.

• Make a shortlist of those overall outlines that you like best. Then forget it for a day. It always pays to take a fresh look at things after a short break.

• If you still like one of your original roughs, begin to work on that, filling in details like paving, surface textures such as gravel, and the position of focal point plants, etc. Leave out planting plans at this stage.

• If your original roughs lack appeal when you look at them again, repeat the process with another batch of ideas. You will probably see ways of improving some of your earlier efforts, so things will be easier this time round.

• If you find it difficult to visualize sizes, peg the design out on the ground with string (see pages 20–21), and modify your plan if necessary.

Finishing Touches

When the outline plan is ready, it's time to fill in the detail and to make sure it will work on the ground. Designs can look very different in actual size and when viewed three-dimensionally rather than as a flatplan on paper. This is the time for fine-tuning, for selecting paving materials, adjusting the plan to minimize the number of cut bricks or slabs, and for visualizing the changes on the ground.

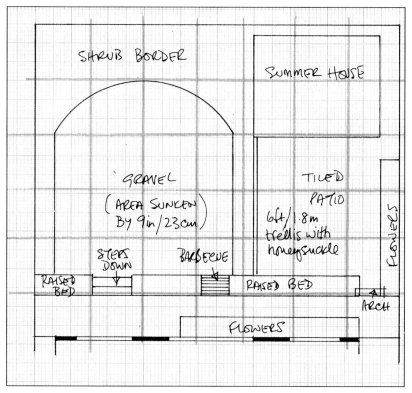

If your design includes irregularly shaped beds, use a length of hose or thick rope to mark out the shape. If you have to cut the beds into an existing lawn, you will need to do this anyway when it's time to start construction.

When the main features and their position have been decided, draw up a detailed plan, such as the one above. It will almost certainly be necessary to make some adjustments to the rough plan to take into account problems on the ground.

In this example, a complicated tile design was chosen for the patio, so the width of the boundary border had to be adjusted so that only half-tiles had to be cut, which would significantly reduce breakages and wastage. This kind of detailed planning can save time, trouble and expense at the construction stage.

Pegging the plan out on the ground also revealed that by keeping to the rectangular pattern, insufficient space would have been left for shrubs at the corners, so these were rounded to provide extra planting space.

Many potential problems can be overcome by critical appraisal and minor adjustments at this stage.

MARKING OUT THE LAYOUT

Curved borders can be marked out with a hose or thick rope, and the curves adjusted so that they look natural and not too acute. Adjustments are easily made by moving the hose or rope until the shape looks right (see above).

If you plan a tree or large shrub, especially where you want it to mask a view or to be seen as a focal point from various parts of the garden, insert a pole or tall cane in the planned position. This will help you to visualize its effect, and you should be able to judge whether shadows cast over other areas are likely to be a problem.

After the design has been marked out on the ground, look at it from as many different angles as possible, and at different times of the day. Provided you choose a sunny day, you will see where shadows fall and where shade could be a problem, but bear in mind that the time of year will affect the angle and length of the shadows. So if you are doing this in the winter, do not be too despondent.

Also, always look at your pegged-out plan from each room that overlooks it. The view from an upstairs room can be particularly useful in helping to visualize the overall plan.

Whenever possible, mark out the layout on the ground – this is the closest you can get to visualizing the finished garden.

Straight lines can be marked out with string stretched between pegs or canes, and an impression of a curve can be achieved by using plenty of pegs or canes close together. Alternatively, use a hose or rope, as described for marking out curved beds. Loose bricks are useful for indicating the outline of raised beds.

The Final Design Plan

No garden design is perfect and you will probably modify it slightly during construction, but it is worth drawing a final scale plan in detail before you order materials and make a physical start. This will enable you to calculate accurately the number of bricks or paving slabs and the amount of other materials (always allow a little extra for wastage).

This is the stage at which you can draw in your planting plans if you prefer. If time and money is limited, it may be better to concentrate on the main construction at this stage, and do the planting later. Much depends on the time of year. If you finish the construction in spring, for example, and want to restrict expenditure on major items like trees and shrubs until the fall or following spring, you can always fill the spaces with cheerful annuals for the first summer at minimal cost. On the other hand, the sooner the long-term plants are put in, the more quickly your garden will have that sought-after mature and established look.

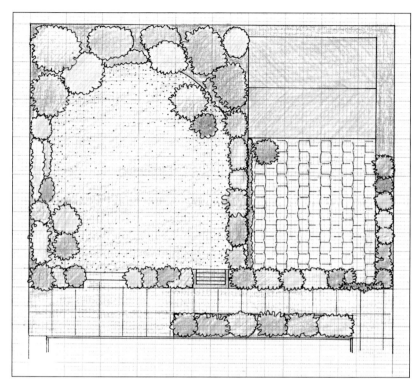

The final plan is the one you will use for construction. Depending on the scale of the plan and size of the garden, you can either mark measurements on the plan or calculate them as necessary from the squared graph paper.

You need not follow your design slavishly – be prepared to modify dimensions and features as appropriate during construction.

Low raised beds can be used to create the effect of enclosed outdoor "rooms" without keeping out light, but in a small area they need to be softened so that they don't dominate the area. Here herbs in containers have been used to add interest and soften the effect of the new walling. Containers like this need not be considered at the planning stage but can be added afterwards.

It will take several seasons for shrubs, climbers, and slow-growing perennials to become established, so fill the gaps with plenty of quick-growing plants for fast results.

Right: *If choosing gravel as a surface, select a type that produces the effect you like. Small pea-sized gravel looks very different from the large, angular gravel used in this picture. The actual effect will also depend on whether the gravel is wet or dry, as well as on the light. Some gravels can look very harsh when dry and viewed in bright sunlight.*

An expanse of gravel can look bleak, so it's a good idea to plant through it if you think the effect needs softening. This can always be done later, and is best improvised rather than planned like a border. Choose plants that grow well in dry conditions.

Preparing a Planting Plan

The hard landscaping acts like a skeleton and gives a garden its structure, but it is the choice of plants that gives it shape and character. Because plants become too large or straggly, or simply die from disease, the weather, or age, planting is an on-going process. But it is always worth starting with a paper plan rather than be influenced by impulse purchase and then wonder where to put the plants.

1 Start with an outline of the area to be planted, with distances marked on the graph paper to make positioning easier, and some good plant books that include plenty of pictures and likely heights and spreads for the plants. Treat likely heights and spreads with caution, as much will depend on soil, seasons, and where you live, but they are a useful guide.

2 If your plant knowledge is good you may be able to draw directly onto your plan, but if you find it easier to move around pieces of paper, cut out shapes to represent the plants that you are planning to include. Write on their height, spread and flowering period if this helps, and mark their name on the back or front.

It will help to color them – evergreen in green, variegated in, say, green and gold stripes, golden plants in yellow, and so on. Colored spots can indicate the color of any flowers. Visual aids like this will help enormously, but bear in mind that flat shapes on paper give no indication of the shapes of the plants (spiky, rounded, feathery, etc.).

Shrubs can be represented as single specimens, but border plants should be planted in groups of threes or fives whenever possible, so that they grow into each other as a drift of color. Be thinking about this when cutting out your shapes.

3 Position the tall or key plants first. You may have to adjust them when the other plants are added, but it is important to get these plants correctly positioned first as they will probably dominate the finished border.

Add the mid-height plants next, but make sure some of these appear to drift towards the back of the border between the taller ones, to avoid the appearance of a rigid, tiered effect.

Finally, fill in with low-growing plants. The larger the drift of these, the more effective they can be. Individual small plants often lack impact, and can be swamped by vigorous neighbors.

4 The initial plans can be fairly crude as they merely explore the possibilities of various plant combinations and associations. So, to visualize the final effect more easily, draw your final planting plan in more detail.

1 CREATING THE OUTLINE

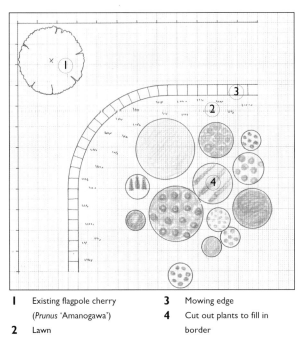

1	Existing flagpole cherry	**3**	Mowing edge
	(*Prunus* 'Amanogawa')	**4**	Cut out plants to fill in
2	Lawn		border

2 ADDING IN THE PLANTS

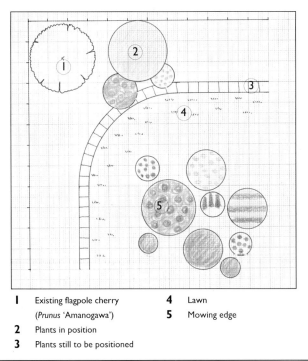

1	Existing flagpole cherry	**4**	Lawn
	(*Prunus* 'Amanogawa')	**5**	Mowing edge
2	Plants in position		
3	Plants still to be positioned		

3 FILLING OUT THE DESIGN

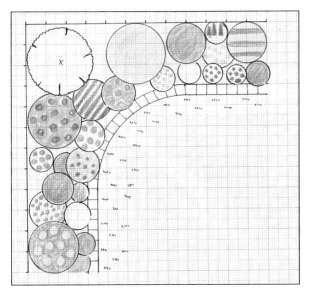

4 COMPLETING THE DETAIL

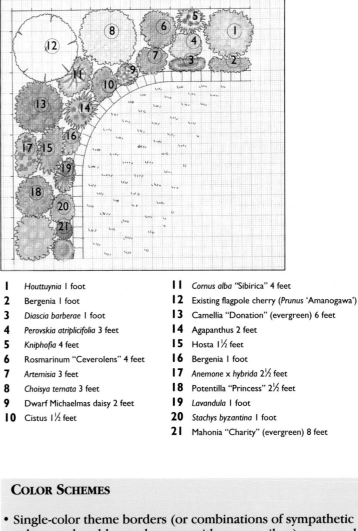

1	*Houttuynia* 1 foot	**11**	*Cornus alba* "Sibirica" 4 feet
2	Bergenia 1 foot	**12**	Existing flagpole cherry (*Prunus* 'Amanogawa')
3	*Diascia barberae* 1 foot	**13**	Camellia "Donation" (evergreen) 6 feet
4	*Perovskia atriplicifolia* 3 feet	**14**	Agapanthus 2 feet
5	*Kniphofia* 4 feet	**15**	Hosta 1½ feet
6	Rosmarinum "Ceverolens" 4 feet	**16**	Bergenia 1 foot
7	*Artemisia* 3 feet	**17**	*Anemone x hybrida* 2½ feet
8	*Choisya ternata* 3 feet	**18**	Potentilla "Princess" 2½ feet
9	Dwarf Michaelmas daisy 2 feet	**19**	*Lavandula* 1 foot
10	*Cistus* 1½ feet	**20**	*Stachys byzantina* 1 foot
		21	Mahonia "Charity" (evergreen) 8 feet

GREEN-FINGERED RULES OF THUMB

• Be careful to insure that tall plants are not placed in front of smaller ones. Heights given in books and catalogs can only be a guide, however, so be prepared for surprises.

• Place tall plants at the back of the border whenever possible (or in the center of an island bed viewed from both sides), but avoid regimented tiers. A few plants that stand above the others in the middle or toward the front of the border often look good.

• Plant herbaceous plants in groups of at least three plants whenever possible. Even in a small area, a group of the same kind of plant will probably have more impact than the same number of plants of different kinds.

• Use plenty of foliage plants – they will remain attractive for much longer than most flowering kinds.

• Do not be afraid to mix shrubs and herbaceous plants – your borders will almost certainly look more interesting all year round. Do not overlook the role of bulbs too, especially bold ones like imperial fritillaries (*Fritillaria imperialis*) and lilies.

• Use plenty of carpeters along the edge and to fill in gaps between large plants. It is better to cover the ground with these than to let weeds grow.

COLOR SCHEMES

• Single-color theme borders (or combinations of sympathetic colors, such as blue and mauve with gray or silver) are popular in large gardens, but difficult to achieve where space is limited and as much variety as possible has to be crammed in.

• If space is limited, it is worth concentrating light-colored plants with golden leaves or foliage that is variegated with a pale color in those parts of the garden that are rather shady and dull.

• If color schemes are important to you, try creating clusters of interesting color combinations or harmonies in parts of the border. A group of three, four or five plants that look good together can have a similar effect to a color-theme border.

Coping with Slopes

Sloping sites are particularly difficult to plan on paper, and they are much more challenging to design in general. It is also more difficult to adapt other people's designs as sloping gardens vary so much in the degree of slope – even whether it is up or down – as well as size and aspect. Sloping gardens really do have to be tailor-made to the site as well as to your preferences. You can, however, turn the drawbacks into advantages, as changes of level can add interest and provide an excellent setting for rock gardens and cascading "streams."

PLANNING A DOWNWARD-SLOPING GARDEN

A downward-sloping garden with an attractive view is much easier to design successfully. The view from the house can be the panorama beyond the garden or the garden itself as it falls away below. If the outlook is unattractive, however, it may be advisable to use the lowest part of the garden, well-screened by shrubs and small trees, as the main sitting area.

The plan on the right demonstrates several important principles when designing a sloping garden, and unusually combines terraces with a natural slope. Terracing is expensive and time-consuming: considerable earth-moving is involved and retaining walls on strong foundations have to be constructed. Likewise, simply moving the topsoil from one area to deposit lower down the slope is unsatisfactory as part of the garden will then be left with subsoil at the surface for planting – a recipe for disappointment. Topsoil should be set aside, the underlying ground levelled, and then the topsoil can be returned.

Terracing provides flat areas on which to walk and relax, and this design includes suitable flat areas along the length of the garden, and as these have been used for hard surfaces, the problem of topsoil movement does not arise. By retaining the natural slope for a large part of the garden, cost and structural work has been reduced.

Although there are some retaining walls, the two walls that zigzag down the garden are stepped so that they remain just above the surrounding ground.

Retaining a large area of naturally sloping ground also provides an ideal setting for rock outcrops and an artificial stream with a series of cascades.

Taking a path across the garden at an angle makes it seem less steep. A path that runs in a straight line down the slope only serves to emphasize the drop.

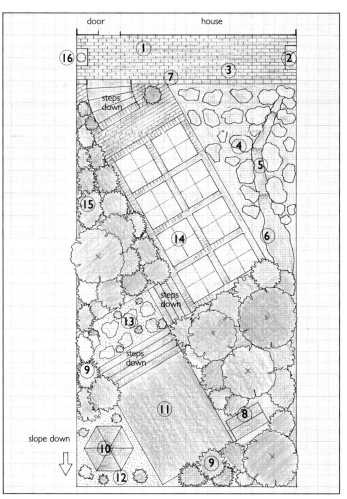

1	Bricks or clay pavers	9	Shrubs
2	Wall fountain with small pool	10	Summerhouse with views across garden and to attractive view below garden
3	Patio		
4	Rock garden bank sloping down-hill and towards flat paved area	11	Lawn
		12	Gravel with alpines
5	"Stream" with cascades	13	Gravel area with natural paving
6	Pond, disappearing behind shrubs	14	Bricks or clay pavers mixed with paving slabs
7	Small retaining wall		
8	House for tools and mower	15	Trees and shrubs
		16	Ornament (on plinth)

AN UPWARD-SLOPING GARDEN

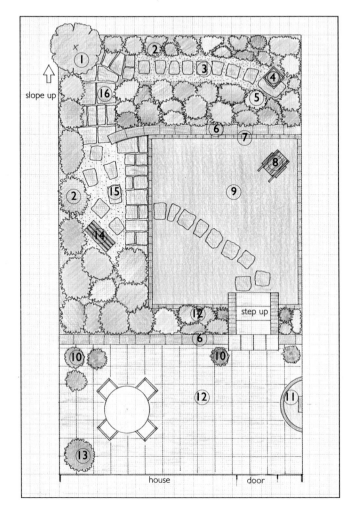

1	Small tree	**9**	Thyme or chamomile lawn
2	Shrubs	**10**	Plants in containers
3	Natural stone paving slabs set in gravel	**11**	Wall fountain with small pool beneath
4	Ornament on plinth as focal point	**12**	Patio
5	Dwarf shrubs on bank	**13**	Shrub or small tree in large tub
6	Retaining wall	**14**	Seat
7	Brick edge	**15**	Natural stone paving slabs set in gravel
8	Lounger or deckchair	**16**	Natural stone path

PLANNING AN UPWARD-SLOPING GARDEN

An upward slope is more challenging. Distant views are not a possibility and even upper floors may look out onto the bank. Terracing can look oppressive, but a "secret" garden full of meandering paths flanked by shrubs is an effective way to deal with the slope. Some retaining walls are usually necessary, but if planted with shrubs, the effect will be masked and the plants on the lower terraces will hide the upper walls and banks.

With this kind of garden it is important to use focal points to give the paths a purpose; just as a maze has a focal point (its center).

Lawns are difficult to accommodate on a steeply sloping site, and difficult to mow too, as mowers are awkward to carry up steps and steep ramps for access. It is generally best to avoid them, but in the example shown left a grass alternative has been used to provide a "lawn" in a small leveled area. The chamomile or thyme only requires an occasional trim with shears, which is not an onerous job for a small area.

Steep slopes are ideal for a rock garden. Construction can be difficult, however, and manhandling and positioning rocks safely on a steep slope requires considerable expertise.

A few rocks will go further if presented as outcrops on a grassy bank, and the effect is more natural and less costly. The drawback is the grass that has to be mown between the rock outcrops; it needs a suitable mower and considerable care taken when cutting.

Long and Narrow

Long, narrow gardens offer great scope for imaginative design. There are opportunities to divide the garden up into a series of smaller gardens or areas with different themes or styles. Instead of a long, narrow lawn with ribbon beds on either side, break it up into a series of areas to be explored and discovered.

Long, narrow gardens, typical of many older town houses, are often laid out with a design that emphasizes their narrowness. Beds that run the length of the garden and long, narrow lawns make the garden predictable and lacking charm. Breaking it up into a series of smaller areas ensures the garden cannot be taken in at a single glance, and it makes it seem cosy and intimate rather than narrow.

The very simple design featured below divides the garden into a series of "rooms," with a trellis and screen-block wall preventing the eye seeing what lies within each section without the oppressiveness of a solid screen.

By including many fragrant shrubs, border plants and annuals in the mixed borders, especially near the garden seats, a fragrant garden can be created, with the scents tending to linger in the enclosed area. The basic design is formal in style, with a long vista leading the eye along to the end of the garden, giving it an impression of size. A simple variation, if you prefer more plants, would be to replace the lawn with border perennials, perhaps mixed with evergreen shrubs.

However you deal with a long, narrow plot, try to break up the garden so that the eye does not go straight down to the end. Make sure there are beds or features that interrupt the straight lines. In this design, two rectangular areas – one paved, the other gravel – have been used to hold interest.

1   Ornament (on plinth)
2   Herb garden
3   Shed
4   Trellis
5   Climbers (e.g., ivy, *parthenocissus* and clematis against trellis)
6   Sundial or birdbath
7   Mixed border
8   Large pot with shrub/shaped clipped box
9   Garden bench
10 Pool with fountain
11 Arch
12 Group of large shrubs (in tubs/large pots)
13 Screen-block wall
14 Patio furniture
15 Vegetable garden
16 Trellis arch
17 Path

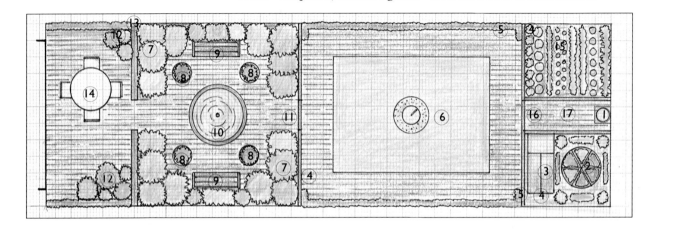

Above: *A focal point toward the center of the garden also helps to distract the eye from the limiting shape of the garden. The role of this attractive planted urn as a focal point is plain to see.*

Left: *Not everyone likes a formal style with lots of straight edges, but you can achieve a similar effect with flowing informal borders and apparently rambling paths.*

In this garden, the borders along the long sides have been extended into broad, curved sweeps, and island beds with conifers have been used to provide visual "blocks."

This kind of design can be achieved quite easily by modifying an existing long, narrow lawn. The beds can be widened with broad sweeps and island beds cut into the grass. Simple paving and planting does the rest. You don't have to spend a lot of money on hard landscaping to create a more interesting garden.

Dealing with Difficult Shapes

Owners of rectangular gardens often wish for a more interesting shape with which to work, but gardens with an irregular shape can be particularly difficult to design. Corner sites are common but surprisingly difficult to use imaginatively, while L-shaped gardens are a special challenge if the two "legs" are to be well-integrated. There are as many solutions as there are gardens with these problems, and the two examples here explore just a few design ideas that you could consider.

AN L-SHAPED GARDEN

If your garden is large, you may prefer to treat the two "legs" separately, perhaps keeping the one visible from the house as an ornamental area, and using the other section as a screened-off kitchen garden, or maybe a more informal wild area planted to attract wildlife. This approach can give you the best of both worlds.

If your garden is relatively small, you will probably want to combine the two areas visually to make the most of available space and to make your garden seem as large as possible. The design shown here uses techniques to make the garden seem as large as possible.

It is important to have a strong design element at the point where the two parts of the garden come together. There must be a reason for walking to the end of the garden so that the remaining part unfolds and entices you to explore.

A seat or an interesting water feature is an ideal focal point, but in this example an arbor as well as a seat has been used, as a pivot around which the two parts of the garden have been centered.

The arbor makes an attractive focal point viewed from any position in the garden, and its rectangular shape helps to "turn" the axis of the garden in a natural and unobtrusive way.

It is desirable to have another focal point at the far end of the garden to make the most of the whole garden.

The arbor effectively "turns" the garden in this design, and manages to look right even though it links two different design styles: the formal rectangular style of house, patio, rectangular lawn and straight-edged flower borders; and the flowing curves of that part of the garden not visible from the house.

Instead of this contrast of styles, you could bring the flower borders that link house with arbor out into the lawn in some gentle curves, or the straight lines of the first section could be carried on into the second. Which option you find most appropriate will be a matter of personal preference.

Instead of an arbor, you could use a summerhouse in the corner, perhaps an octagonal one so that it does not appear to have just one "front," set in the corner. This would make a strong focal point, and from it you could enjoy the view along both sections of your garden.

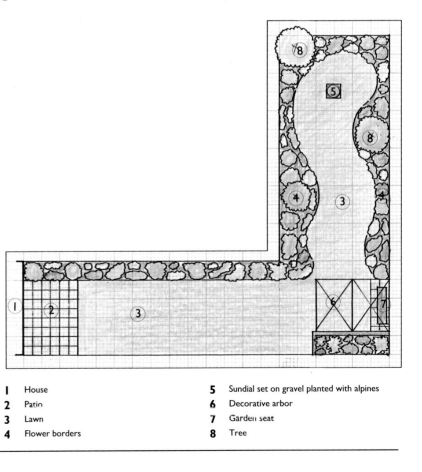

1	House	5	Sundial set on gravel planted with alpines
2	Patio	6	Decorative arbor
3	Lawn	7	Garden seat
4	Flower borders	8	Tree

A CORNER SITE

Corner sites offer lots of scope, but they can be rather "public" unless screened in some way with a fence or hedge. Always check whether this is permissible, however, as there may be restrictions in the deeds of the property or specified by the local zoning rules concerning the height of hedges, etc., if they are likely to obstruct the view for traffic. Usually, however, you can create a sense of privacy and still keep within any restrictions there may be.

If you want something more intensively designed than, say, a lawn that sweeps around the house, it is worth trying to create a design that integrates the two sides. In this example, a design based on a grid diagonal to the house has been used to take full advantage of the long dimension across the garden, while at the same time using shrubs to mask the curved boundary, which also gives privacy.

If this highly structured design does not appeal to you, a more informal style with lawn and sweeping beds could be used.

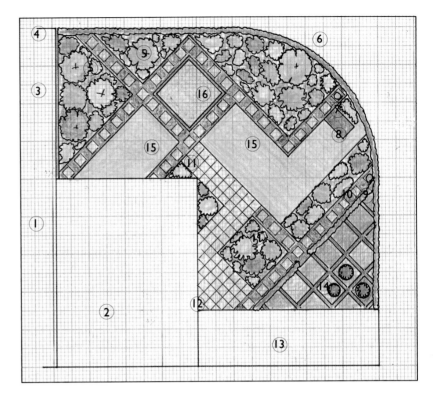

1	Back garden	9	Dwarf hedge
2	House	10	Shrubs and border plants
3	Screen-block wall	11	Plants
4	Gate	12	Front door
5	Shrubs	13	Driveway
6	Hedge	14	Colored slabs and plants in containers
7	Ornament	15	Lawn
8	Garden seat	16	Pond

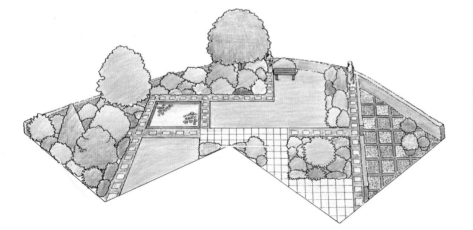

In this design it is the paths that lay the foundation for the diagonal pattern, so they have been given strong visual impact. As continuous paving slabs would look boring as well as uninspiring, they have been spaced and set into a wider area of gravel. By using fine or coarse gravel, or even small shingle, the character of the paths can be changed to suit individual preference.

The extra depth given to the planting areas by their angular shape provides scope for planting small trees or large specimen shrubs to add height and a greater sense of structure.

Outdoor Rooms

Your garden will be much more interesting if it cannot all be seen at once. Whether you have an entirely different style in each area (for example, a wild border or a romantic, secluded corner) or variations on the basic theme, the more it has to be explored, like the rooms of a house, the more fascinating it becomes.

This principle also applies to a small garden, when it can be even more valuable as a design technique. A small garden, such as the one shown here, where everything can be taken in at a quick glance, is likely to be boring, but if you have to go around a few screens, negotiate a few bends or obstacles, it will hold many more surprises.

Right: *As the photograph shows, this garden is narrow, but sometimes even a narrow garden can be divided in both directions. This avoids the banded effect that would result if all the divisions were horizontal across the garden with no vertical divisions to balance them out.*

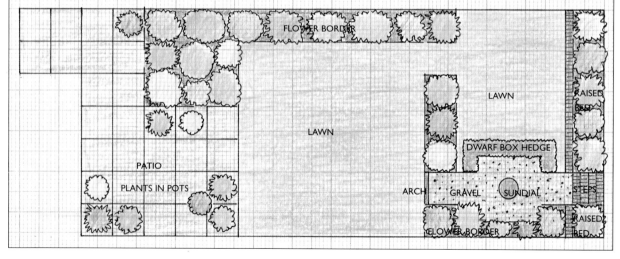

FLOWER BORDER

LAWN

RAISED BED

LAWN

DWARF BOX HEDGE

PATIO

PLANTS IN POTS

ARCH GRAVEL SUNDIAL STEPS

FLOWER BORDER

RAISED BED

Left: *In plan view the simplicity of this design is obvious, yet the slight changes of level and height provided by shrubs and the low hedge all help to give the impression of moving from room to room, with a series of gardens within the garden.*

Left: *By placing the arch and the steps at the end of the garden off-center, a vista has been produced that runs along the whole length of the garden, as seen from the patio. This gives the garden a sense of depth and size, even though areas have been partitioned off for individual exploration.*

Above: *Raised beds and a graveled area add more variety and a sense of enclosure, and provide a good point from which to view the garden, as the picture shows. The small graveled area would have been impractical as grass, but the gravel is an ideal surface for this situation. Different surface textures are important in creating the sense of walking into different areas.*

In Cottage-garden Style

Cottage gardens are by nature undefinable, yet a garden with the attributes of a cottage garden is instantly recognizable. The emphasis is on dense planting, with a bias towards perennial border plants, and the "design" lies more in the planting than the structure of the garden. They usually look uninspiring in plan view – frequently two wide borders with a path down the middle between gate and door. If your interest lies more in the plants than the hard landscaping, a cottage-garden style could be the solution.

A typical cottage garden is extremely simple in design – often straight, but wide, borders and little else. If your garden is squat, square, and small, you can create a similar effect by treating the whole area like a large border, with a path running around the edge.

To create the appropriate period atmosphere, keep to species or early hybrids rather than highly-bred plants that look too modern. Delphiniums, oriental poppies and achilleas, along with plants such as border pinks and lady's-mantle (*Alchemilla*) were commonplace in country gardens and will help to create the style and "atmosphere" that you are seeking.

An old building and roses around the door clearly help, but you can create cottage garden borders in a modern setting if you use another part of the garden, rather than the house, as a backdrop.

In the garden shown here, the plants are all border perennials – in effect large herbaceous borders – but traditionally there would be lots of annuals such as calendulas and love-in-a-mist (Nigella damascena) *too.*

PLANTING SUGGESTIONS

Use the two schemes opposite as a guide for your own cottage garden border. Do not follow them slavishly, but add plants that you prefer (provided they are appropriate), and drop those that you do not like. Each of these borders is approximately 12 feet by 6 feet, so you may have to drop some plants if your border is smaller. The borders are shown as mature, with clumps of border perennials that have been established for some years – you may be able to accommodate the same number of plants in a smaller space if you lift and divide more frequently.

In many cases, more than one plant is represented by the areas shown in the borders opposite (border plants are generally best planted in groups of three to five of each kind if there is space). The lupines, for example, represent a bold drift of a number of plants.

These are just some of the cottage garden plants that you could use: there are many more. Remember to keep to types that would have been around, say, 50 years ago or more: do not use modern hybrid lilies in place of the *Lilium regale* shown here, for example.

Hardy perennials shown in the borders include aquilegia, bear's-breech (*Acanthus mollis*), bee balm (*Monarda didyma*), bleeding-heart (*Dicentra spectabilis*), catmint (*Nepeta*), coral-bells (*Heuchera sanguinea*), delphinium, iris, gaillardia, geum, small globe thistle (*Echinops ritro*), hollyhock, lady's-mantle (*Alchemilla*), lupine, Michaelmas daisy, oriental poppy (*Papaver orientale*), herbaceous peony, perennial gypsophila, pinks, pyrethrum, red hot poker (*kniphofia*), regal lily (*Lilium regale*), sea holly (*Eryngium maritimum*), daisy (*Leucanthemum x superbum*), sneezewort (*Achillea ptarmica*), viola and fernleaf yarrow (*Achillea filipendulina*).

Biennials used are Canterbury-bells and foxgloves. Annuals are cornflowers, pot-marigolds (*Calendula*), sunflowers (*Helianthus*), and Virginia-stocks (*Malcolmia maritima*).

COTTAGE BORDER PLAN A

1   Delphinium
2   Daisy (*Leucanthemum* x *superbum*)
3   Gypsophila
4   Gaillardia
5   Pyrethrum
6   Pinks or border carnations (*Dianthus*)
7   Bearded iris
8   Red hot poker (*Kniphofia*)
9   Aquilegia
10   Pot-marigolds (Calendula)
11   Coral-bells
12   Regal lily
13   Hollyhock
14   Michaelmas daisy (*Aster*)
15   Crocosmia
16   Canterbury-bells (*Campanula*)
17   Virginia-stocks (*Malcomia*)
18   Viola cornuta
19   Sneezewort (*Achillea ptarmica*)

COTTAGE BORDER PLAN B

1a   Delphinium
2a   Foxglove (*Digitalis*)
3a   Fernleaf yarrow (*Achillea filipendulina*)
4a   Geum
5a   Catmint (*Nepeta*)
6a   Lupine
7a   Small globe thistle (*Echinops*)
8a   Oriental poppy (*Papaver*)
9a   Peony
10a   Sea holly (*Eryngium*)
11a   Cornflower (*Centaurea*)
12a   Lavender (*Lavendula*)
13a   Bleeding-heart (*Dicentra spectabilis*)
14a   Lady's-mantle (*Alchemilla*)
15a   Bee balm (*Monarda didyma*)
16a   Bearded iris
17a   Bear's-breech (*Acanthus*)
18a   Sunflowers (*Helianthus*)

In Formal Style

Privacy and seclusion is something most of us appreciate at some time, and it can be even more precious when we are relaxing in the garden. Even in a country garden without overlooking neighbors, it is nice to have a cosy and secluded corner that feels snug and enclosed, but in a town or city it may be the whole garden that needs to be encapsulated in its own private "cocoon", a private green oasis among the surrounding buildings.

There are two fundamental approaches to a courtyard or tiny town garden: the formal one that depends on structures such as walls for privacy, like the one shown on the opposite page (*top*), or an informal approach that depends on the lush growth of trees and shrubs. The illustration on page 37 (*bottom*) is a good example of a garden designed with this approach: the sitting area in the center is like a clearing in woodland.

This type of dense planting with tall-growing shrubs and small trees can become very shady in summer, but on a hot day this can be a welcome attribute. It is also a great way to enjoy a lot of plants in a small area – provided you are willing to cut back and prune fairly ruthlessly on a regular basis, you can pack in a surprising number of plants in a small area, but concentrate on shade-lovers.

Often, however, it's impossible to pretend that your garden is anywhere other than in a town or city, surrounded by other buildings, in which case a formal style that makes a bold and challenging statement despite its surroundings is a pleasing solution.

Tall walls are an asset. They have a sense of age and permanence that a fence never gives, and they can be taller. If well constructed and wide, you can even stand pots and finials on top, especially where there are supporting columns. Walls also provide an ideal support for climbers and for trained fruit or ornamental wall shrubs.

Whether you want to draw attention to the tops of the walls with ornaments or plants will depend on the background. If it is particularly unattractive, it is advisable to draw the eye down into the garden and not upwards to its perimeter.

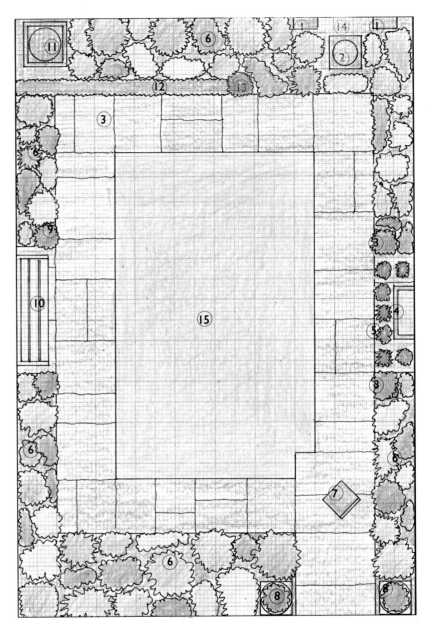

1	Pillars covered with ivy and topped with finials	8	Clipped box in pots on plinths
2	Urn on pedestal	9	Box spiral
3	Natural paving stones	10	White garden seat
4	Wall fountain	11	Large urn on pedestal
5	Box balls in pots	12	Dwarf box hedge
6	Border plants	13	Clipped and shaped box
7	Garden chair	14	Decorative trellis covering old gate
		15	Lawn

Left: *If you decide on a classical or period style like this, it is advisable to use materials that do it justice. There is not a lot of hard land-scaping, so be prepared to pay for natural stone paving, and invest in a few ornaments that do the garden justice. Trained and clipped box like these specimens can be expensive, but you will not have to spend much on shrubs for the rest of the garden. And because there are few areas for which you will have to buy seasonal plants, the ongoing costs will be minimal.*

Right: *The designer here has chosen a strong rectangular theme for the paved area, to contrast with the luxuriant and overhanging plants that soften the straight lines. The choice of plain square slabs, arranged in unstaggered rows, gives the design a simple uncluttered appearance.*

Opposite page: *The essentials of this design plan are simplicity and restraint, with the emphasis on shape and form provided by the urns and shaped box plants. Add touches of seasonal color in small containers that can be moved around the garden to suit the season and the mood.*

The Herb Garden

No garden is complete without its complement of herbs, and finding a suitable place for them should be considered at the planning stage. A special herb garden is ideal, and can be a highly decorative feature, but many herbs make good container plants, and many are pretty enough to be grown in borders along with the ornamentals. You can simply grow herbs in the kitchen garden together with the vegetables, but why not make more of a feature of them?

A formal herb garden divided into "compartments", like the one featured on the right, is practical and a powerful focal point. Separating the various herbs makes cultivation much easier, as some are annuals, some perennials, some self-seed prolifically and, if surrounded by soil, can become weeds, and others have spreading roots or stems that benefit from containment.

The suggested planting in this plan should be treated only as a starting point for your own choice. There is little point in growing herbs that you do not use unless they are particularly decorative. If you use a lot of one kind of herb, allocate more than one area. There is space for 24 different herbs in this design, but you may prefer to grow only the dozen that you use most often and create a mirror image in the two halves of the herb garden.

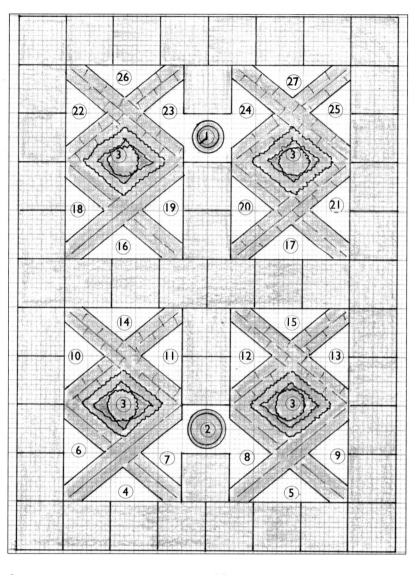

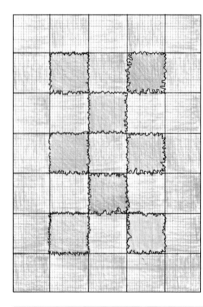

Left: *A checkerboard herb garden can be very effective for a paved area. It has a strong visual impact, and you can easily keep each herb contained within its own small plot while still being able to walk among them.*

1	Sundial	14	Winter savory
2	Birdbath	15	Lavender
3	Dwarf box hedge with bay in center	16	Thyme
	Suggested planting	17	Borage
4	Summer savory	18	Chives
5	Variegated lemon balm	19	Golden marjoram
6	Variegated apple mint	20	Rosemary
7	Purple sage	21	Mint
8	Lavender cotton	22	Caraway
9	Parsley	23	Bergamot
10	Hyssop	24	Sweet basil
11	French tarragon	25	Chervil
12	Sorrel	26	Garlic
13	Oregano	27	Pot-marigold (*Calendula*)

Left: *The herb garden can become a decorative part of the overall garden design. Bear in mind that herb gardens can be quiescent in winter, however, as most of the plants will have died down, so they are best used to create interest in a part of the garden that you suddenly discover. Most herbs prefer to be in full sun, so try to choose a position that is in good light for most of the day.*

Below: *There's always space for a few herbs, even if you have to put them in containers. This group of pots contains chives, French tarragon and winter savory.*

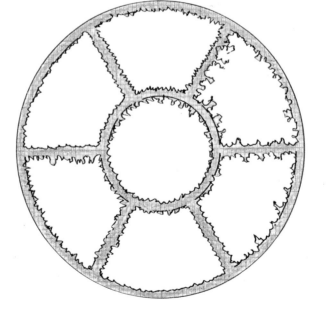

Above: *Where space is limited, a herb wheel is a popular choice. Proper cart wheels can be used, but as these are hard to obtain, a similar effect can be achieved with the use of bricks. Plant a different herb in each space created by the spokes.*

The Kitchen Garden

The traditional kitchen garden demands little design but lots of planning for crop positioning and rotation. Usually an area out of sight of the main ornamental part of the garden is set aside and the crops are grown in straight rows. This simplifies crop rotation and makes cultivation easier – you can weed more easily between straight rows, and it is simpler to give each specific crop the appropriate fertilizer and supplementary water when it is required. If you want to make vegetable growing a more high-profile part of your garden, however, you may have to be bold.

Dedicated areas set aside for traditional rows of vegetables make cultivation relatively simple, but integrating flowers and vegetables can be an interesting experiment. It also may help reduce the level of pest and disease infestation that often comes with large areas devoted to a small range of plants.

A potager is a striking way to combine vegetables and flowers, and though expensive to construct and time-intensive to maintain (lots of dwarf box hedging to plant and clip, for instance), it can be justified if it forms a main feature. In a large garden you can enclose the area with hedges, but in a small garden you may want to make this the whole of your design. This is most likely to appeal if your interest lies as much in cooking and a love of fresh vegetables as in ornamental gardening.

The term *jardin potager* is French for "kitchen garden," but the word "potager" has come to mean primarily a kitchen garden that usually contains both vegetables and fruit, laid out ornamentally and often with the beds edged with low hedges like a parterre.

On the other hand, the traditional vegetable plot can be improved simply by giving it a structure with paths. The design on the right is ideal if you want to practice the 4-foot-bed "no-dig" system, where cultivation is done by reaching across from the paths so that the soil is not compacted.

1 Flower border around edge	**4** Topiary shapes
2 Ornament	**5** Large clipped box
3 Dwarf box hedge	**6** Gate/entrance

This design is a more decorative vegetable plot. The use of an ornament such as a birdbath or sundial in the center emphasizes the formality of this type of vegetable garden.

In a potager like this, you can devote the main beds purely to vegetables, and even grow them in straight rows in the conventional manner, but if you want to be bold, try growing flowers and vegetables together.

Many vegetables are ornamental enough to be used in flower borders, among bedding plants, and even in containers – like this rhubarb chard sharing a half-barrel with lobelia.

This method of growing vegetables, some in rows, others interplanted more randomly with flowers, may not appeal, but breaking up the usual solid blocks may actually assist with insect control.

Mixing vegetables, herbs and flowers, will make your vegetable plot full of surprises, and interesting too.

ORNAMENTAL VEGETABLES

- Where space is really restricted, and there is insufficient room for a vegetable garden, or it is inadequate for the amount that you wish to grow, try growing some of the more decorative vegetables among the flowers.

- This has drawbacks of course – there may be gaps when harvesting time arrives. This may not be a problem if you use the vegetables as gap fillers though, and the surrounding plants grow to fill the space left after harvesting.

- Beets, carrots and rhubarb chard are all decorative foliage plants. Use them to help to fill in gaps in beds and borders, but don't forget that you still have to thin them, even though they are grown in clusters or groups rather than rows.

- Lettuces can be attractive until they run to seed, especially red varieties. The best ones to use are the "cut-and-come again" types such as "Salad Bowl" and "Oak-leaf," because you can harvest the leaves without destroying the whole plant and leaving a gap.

Creating the Garden Structure

Important though an overall design is, it is individual features that make a garden special. Deciding whether to have a patio, pond or path, and if so, of what sort, will have a significant impact on the feel of the garden as a whole. Even smaller details, such as ornaments, furniture and lighting, can make a real difference, so it is worth taking time to devise the best combination of structural features.

Left: *This quiet corner has been transformed by a white-painted trellis and seat.*

Above: *Attractive effects can be achieved simply – these bricks give a formal air to the flower bed.*

Lawns

A lawn is time- and energy-consuming but if you don't want to get rid of what is often the centerpiece of the garden, there are legitimate – and attractive – ways to reduce the frequency with which you have to mow.

Simply mowing different areas of the lawn to different heights, to create a textured effect can achieve a significant time saving but needs a fairly large lawn for the best effect. Naturalizing spring-flowering bulbs in a lawn of any size gives you the justification for leaving the grass uncut until late spring or early summer, when the leaves have died down.

A wild-flower lawn will bring many insect, animal and bird visitors to your garden, and regular mowing will be unnecessary. This kind of lawn can look untidy at times, so it's more suitable for the back garden than the front.

NATURALIZING BULBS IN GRASS

Choose bulbs that will multiply and flower freely, such as crocuses, daffodils, snowdrops, small fritillaries, and winter aconites. There are many different kinds of crocuses and daffodils, so you'll have plenty of choice even if you limit yourself to these particularly reliable bulbs and corms.

Above right: *Hyacinth bulbs will make bold drifts if left undisturbed for several years, and there is the bonus of the flowers' fragrance.*

1 For large bulbs, such as daffodils, scatter the bulbs randomly then make individual holes with a bulb planter (or use a trowel). Most bulbs planters are designed so that the core of soil is easily released.

2 Place the bulb into the hole, making sure there isn't a large air pocket beneath it, then return the core of grass. It may be necessary to remove a little soil from the bottom of the core for a snug fit. Firm the grass gently back into place.

3 For small bulbs or corms such as crocuses, you can lift an area of grass instead. Make an H-shaped cut with a spade blade or edging tool, and fold back the turf. Then fork in a little slow-acting fertilizer such as bonemeal.

4 Scatter the bulbs or corms randomly and leave very small ones where they fall. Larger ones may need planting with a trowel. Level and firm the soil, then return the grass. Firm it in carefully to ensure the ground remains level.

A WILDLIFE HAVEN

You can encourage birds, butterflies and other creatures by having a wild-flower lawn instead of a conventional lawn. You may still want to retain a grass lawn for practical purposes, but some of the area can be allowed to "go wild", especially if the area is not on public view.

1 The most satisfactory way to make a wild-flower lawn is to sow a special wild-flower mixture instead of lawn seed. Be sure to remove problem perennial weeds first.

Above: *An area like this, full of wild flowers, can look drab at certain times of the year, but is enchanting when the plants are in bloom.*

2 To bury the seeds, simply rake first in one direction and then in the other. It does not matter if some seeds remain on the surface. Keep the area well watered until the seeds germinate.

3 For a very small area, you may prefer to buy wild-flower plants, which are now sold by some garden centers. You can also raise your own plants, starting them off in seed trays or pots.

4 You can plant into bare ground or put them in an area of lawn left to grow long. Don't forget to keep them well watered until established.

THE ANNUAL HAIRCUT

A wild-flower lawn cannot simply be left uncut, or it will become an untidy wilderness. Cut the area down to within a few inches of the ground in the autumn or when most of the flowers have finished blooming and have shed their seeds. This will make it look tidier for the winter, and new growth next spring will not become entangled with old growth.

Cut the Mowing Time Down to Size

There's a lot you can do to keep mowing time to a minimum. It may be necessary to buy a new and better mower, but just cutting out fussy beds, and curved edges might simplify and speed things up by allowing you to mow up and down in straight lines. Or you can take a sideways look at the problem and cut different parts of the lawn at different intervals, leaving some areas longer.

KEEP A STRAIGHT LINE

Beds cut into the lawn will probably increase mowing time. Although they reduce the area of lawn, the inability to mow up and down in straight lines will probably slow you down. Creating a striped finish is particularly difficult and beds also create more edges to trim. Consider filling them in with grass or at least making them into rectangles.

KEEP A STRAIGHT EDGE

Untrimmed edges can make a garden look untidy, but trimming with long-handled shears – or especially with ordinary shears – is tedious and time-consuming.

If you have a lot of lawn edges to trim, buy a powered lawn edger, or choose a nylon line trimmer with a swivel head that can be used for this job as well as cutting down weeds.

Above: *A curved bed will add considerably to mowing time, as you will not be able to mow in a straight line.*

Above: *A nylon line trimmer will enable you to trim edges with considerable speed.*

MULTI-LEVEL MOWING

Another way to cut down on the mowing for a large lawn is to create a "sculptured" effect. Keep the broad "pathways" cut regularly, cut other areas with the blade set higher, and mow only every second or third time. Leave some uncut except for a couple of times a season. However, do remember that very long grass can't easily be cut with a mower; you'll need to get out your nylon line trimmer.

Above: *If the lawn is large, try leaving the grass in part of it to grow long. Wild flowers will start to thrive, and you will only need to cut it once a year.*

MAKE A MOWING EDGE

If you have a mowing edge like this, edge-trimming will be required much less often. If the edging is set level with the grass, the mower, which is run onto the edging, will trim off the long grass at the edge. You may still have to trim any spreading grass stems that grow over the paving, but this will only be necessary occasionally.

I Lay the paving slabs on the grass for positioning, and use a half-moon edger (edging iron) to cut a new edge.

2 Slice off the grass with a spade, and remove enough soil for a couple of inches of sand and gravel mix, mortar, and the slabs. Consolidate the sub-base.

3 Use five blobs of mortar on which to bed the slab, and tap the paving level, using a mallet or the handle of a club hammer.

4 Make sure the slabs are flush with the lawn, and use a spirit level to check that the slabs are laid evenly. Mortar the joints for a neat finish, otherwise weeds will grow in them.

Above: *Bricks can be used instead of paving slabs, and in a formal setting these can give an attractive crisp finish to the bed.*

CUT WIDE, SAVE TIME

Next time you buy a mower, think about the cutting width. Wider mowers cost a little more but will save time. But think carefully first – if your lawn is very small the saving may not be significant and the extra maneuverability of a smaller mower can be important if there are few long straight runs.

Alternatives to Grass

If you like a green lawn, but don't enjoy the regular grass cutting, why not try a grass substitute? None of those suggested here will stand up to the hard wear of a children's play area like grass, but just for occasional foot traffic and as a feature that is for admiration only, there are some practical alternatives that don't need regular mowing.

THYME

Thyme is aromatic when crushed, and makes a good grass substitute, but don't use the culinary thyme (*Thymus vulgaris*), which is too tall. Choose a carpeter like *T. pseudolanuginosus* or *T. serpyllum*.

CHAMOMILE

Chamomile (*Chamaemelum nobile*, syn. *Anthemis nobilis*) is also aromatic and looks good too. Look for the variety 'Treneague', which is compact and does not normally flower.

CLOVER

If clover is a problem in your lawn, it may make a good grass substitute. Once established it will keep green for most of the year, and will tolerate dry soils. You'll only have to mow a couple of times a year, after the flowers appear, to keep it looking fit. You will need to order clover seed from a seed company that sells wild or agricultural seeds.

PLANTING A THYME LAWN

You must prepare the ground thoroughly and eliminate as many weeds as possible otherwise weeding will become a tiresome chore. Time spent now will be time saved later.

1 Prepare the ground thoroughly by digging over the area and levelling it at least a month before planting. This will allow the soil to settle and weed seedlings to germinate.

2 Dig out any deep-rooted perennial weeds that appear. Hoe out seedlings. Rake level again.

3 Water all the plants in their pots first, then set them out about 8 in apart, in staggered rows as shown (a little closer for quicker cover, a little further apart for economy but slower cover).

4 Knock the plant from its pot and carefully tease out a few of the roots if they are running tightly around the edge of the pot.

5 Plant at their original depth, and firm the soil around the roots before planting the next one.

CHEAP PLANTS

Pot-grown plants from a garden center can be expensive if you need a great number. You can cut the cost by buying some plants and using these for cuttings. Grow them on for a year before planting. Some thymes are easily raised from seed, but start them off in seed trays then grow on in pots for a season.

BEWARE THE PITFALLS

Grass substitutes have drawbacks as well as advantages. You won't be able to use selective lawn weedkillers on them, so it's back to old-fashioned hand weeding. Once the new lawn is well established and the plants have knitted together this will not be a major problem, but weeding will be a chore for the first season or two.

Beware of common stonecrop (*Sedum acre*), an attractive yellow-flowered carpeter sometimes sold as a grass-substitute. It looks great, but it will probably become a serious weed in your garden. You will almost certainly regret its introduction.

6 Water the ground thoroughly and keep well watered for the first season.

Right: *Thymes make an attractive alternative to grass if the area is small and is unlikely to take much wear.*

Gravel Gardens

Gravel is great if you want an easy-to-lay, trouble-free surface that looks good and harmonizes well with plants. It's worth getting to know your gravels, especially if you're looking for practical alternatives to a lawn.

Right: *Many garden centers and stone merchants sell, or can obtain, a wide range of gravels in different sizes and colors. You will find the appearance changes according to the light and whether the stones are wet or dry.*

MAKING A GRAVEL GARDEN

Gravel is an easy and inexpensive material to work with, and a small gravel garden can be created in a weekend.

Below: *Gravel gardens can be a formal or informal shape, but an edging of some kind is required otherwise the gravel will become scattered into surrounding beds.*

1 Excavate the area to a depth of about 4 in, with a slight slope to avoid waterlogging after heavy rain. If the gravel garden is low-lying or in a hollow, provide a sump for excess water to drain into.

2 Make sure the surface is reasonably smooth, then lay thick plastic sheeting over the area (to suppress weed growth). Overlap the joints.

3 Tip the gravel over the plastic sheet, and rake it level. It is difficult to judge how deeply or evenly the gravel is being spread once the plastic sheet has been covered, so if necessary scrape back the gravel occasionally to check progress.

4 If you want to plant through the gravel, scoop back the gravel to expose the plastic sheet. Then make cross-slits through the plastic with a knife.

5 Make the planting hole with a trowel, enrich the soil with garden compost and fertilizer and plant normally. Fold back the sheet, and replace the gravel without covering the crown if it's a small plant.

Patio Pleasures

Patios are popular because they bridge the gap between house and garden, and even though they are sometimes located remotely from the house, they provide an opportunity to "live" in the garden. They are great for entertaining, and are a perfect place to sit, relax and admire the rest of your garden. Patios are for people, but they should be places for plants too. Be prepared to spend time planning a patio that will look beautiful and not boring. The more "room-like" you make it, the more inviting it will be as a place to relax or entertain.

Situating a patio next to the house, with adjoining patio doors or French windows, integrates house and garden and makes it an extension of the living area. Choosing a surface such as wooden decking or glazed tiles also helps to tie it more closely as an extension of the house in a way that is difficult to achieve with paving slabs or clay pavers.

If a room opens onto the patio, it is more practical to use stylish and upholstered chairs as they can easily be moved indoors at the end of the day.

Sometimes, however, simplicity is appropriate, especially if the patio is located away from the house. An area paved with bricks or clay pavers often blends more sympathetically with the surrounding garden than concrete blocks or slabs, and if any pillars for a patio overhead are made from bricks, the design will look well-integrated and carefully planned.

In a large garden, setting the patio at a 45-degree angle to the house can be very effective. It helps to join two sides of the garden, while at the same time linking house and garden over a broad angle. In this example, the angle has been emphasized by the use of rows of bricks that take the eye across the patio.

Mixing materials, such as bricks and paving slabs, creates a more interesting surface texture than using just one kind of paving. Do not use more than three different kinds of paving, however; otherwise the effect may look fussy and confused.

The more "room-like" you can make a patio, the cosier and more intimate it will appear as a place to sit and relax or to entertain friends. Useful techniques to use are a wall to give a sense of enclosure and a change of level or a "gateway" to the rest of the garden. Paving that simply butts onto the lawn at the same level tends to look lifeless, and the patio lacks impact because it has no clear-cut boundary.

When not actually used for entertaining, this kind of paved area is often best furnished with just a few simple, but elegant, chairs. The use of space can bring its own sense of tranquillity.

An abundant use of containers helps to make a patio look furnished and welcoming, but they add considerably to the maintenance required. Patio plants should always look in tip-top condition, which demands regular watering, feeding and removing faded flowers.

TIPS FOR A PERFECT PATIO

• Make sure it is large enough to be able to move around freely, even when you have a few guests. If it is heavily planted and has a lot of furniture, you may need to allow a little extra space.

• Choose a sunny position, away from overhanging trees (insects, leaves and drips after a shower can all be problems).

• Provide shelter from wind. If on an exposed site, or near a wind tunnel – perhaps between houses – provide a windbreak. A screen block wall, with shrubs in front, can be decorative and will filter the wind. Solid brick walls can look oppressive if tall, but a low wall can be useful, as you are often less exposed when sitting.

• Give your patio clear boundaries – a low wall or a raised bed, even an ornamental hedge or dwarf shrubs can be used. If the patio is large, a balustrade can look impressive. A simple change of level, with a step up or down to the rest of the garden, is a good way to create the illusion of a boundary while maintaining a seamless link with the rest of the garden.

• Consider having a pergola over-head, especially if the patio adjoins the house. This can provide shade in summer if it is covered with a vine or climber (nothing with spines or long, cascading shoots however).

Paths and Paving

Paths and areas of paving such as patios give the garden its backbone and shape. While seasonal plants are momentarily spectacular, they come and go, but the hard surfacing remains as a year-round reminder of the basic garden design, and will show up its strengths and weaknesses. It is worth spending time, thought and money on getting the framework of paths and paving right.

Concrete paving blocks remain a popular choice because they are readily available in a wide range of finishes and are much cheaper than natural stone alternatives. The formal and regular shape needs to be offset by lavish planting that spills over the edges to create a soft, well-clothed look. A neutral color is often more successful than a mixture of bright colors (which soon become uniformly dull anyway with age). Small sizes usually look best in a small area, and are easier to handle and lay.

LAYING BRICKS AND CLAY PAVERS

1 If a path will have to take heavy use, bed bricks on mortar, but for paths only subject to occasional foot traffic you can bed them on sand, like clay pavers. In either case, prepare a sound and stable sub-base.

2 Lay several rows of bricks, then tap them flat using a mallet or the handle of a club hammer over a straight-edged piece of wood. On a narrow path you will not need to build in a slight fall, but on a large area such as for a patio, this will be necessary to ensure water drains away freely.

3 The easiest way to mortar the joints between bricks is to brush in a dry mix, pressing it down between the bricks with a small piece of wood to eliminate large air pockets.

4 Finally, spray with water from a compression sprayer or a watering-can fitted with a fine rose. Apply just enough water to clean the surface of the bricks and moisten between the joints. If necessary, clean off any mortar stains with a damp cloth before they dry.

In parts of the garden where the path is not subject to regular heavy use, a more random appearance can be satisfying, and if you allow a few suitable plants to meander between and around the paving, the effect can be very pleasing.

Even in a small area, mixing materials and providing strong lines will create a positive impression of imaginative design. In this garden, the main surfacing materials are concrete paving slabs and gravel, but they have been separated by old railroad ties that add a contrast of texture and color. A garden area like this will remain attractive even when the summer plants have died down.

Even small paths leading to odd corners of the garden deserve careful thought. This short path that leads from the main garden to a wooden seat, has been made into a feature as strong as the borders that flank it or the seat that it leads to. If only rectangular paving slabs had been used, it would have been unremarkable and uninteresting, but the addition of a few patterned pavers and pebbles has managed to transform it into a distinctive path packed with interest.

Plants and Paving

Make your paved areas more interesting by mixing materials, and leaving plenty of space for plants. That way it will always remain high on impact and still low on maintenance.

PLANTING IN PAVING

A large expanse of paving needs some plants to soften the effect. Keep containers to a minimum unless you have an automatic watering system. Instead, try lifting a few paving slabs and plant straight into these prepared areas. The effect will be similar but with much less commitment than containers demand.

MIX AND MATCH MATERIALS

Paving often looks a more integrated part of the garden if you combine it with raised beds or low walls made from the same or matching materials – but always check that bricks used for walls are suitable for paths as well.

Using the same or matching paving for paths and patios is another way of giving your garden a more integrated look.

If the area is large, try mixing materials. Using two or three different materials usually works well, but more than three is likely to look confused. Try bricks or clay pavers with timber, or railway sleepers, or natural or man-made paving slabs. You could perhaps leave out some areas of paving and fill them with gravel or pebbles.

Above right: *This paved area is combined with a raised bed made from contrasting materials.*

1 Lift one or two paving slabs, using a cold chisel or bolster with a club hammer to break the mortar and lift the slabs.

2 Remove the mortar and any hardcore, then fork in several buckets of garden compost or a proprietary planting mix, together with a handful of slow-release fertilizer.

3 Plant the shrub normally, firming the soil around the roots and watering thoroughly. Keep well watered in dry weather for the first season.

4 Beach pebbles or gravel may be used to cover the soil and make it look more attractive. This also reduces the chance of soil splashing onto the paving.

ADDING PEBBLE TEXTURE

1 Beach pebbles (you can buy these from some builder's merchants, garden centers and stone merchants) are a good way to create an area of different texture. Leave out as many slabs as appropriate and fill the area with a dryish mortar mix. Then lay the stones close together.

2 If the area is likely to be walked over, make sure the stones are flush with the surrounding paving. Use a stout piece of wood laid across adjoining slabs to ensure they are flush and reasonably level. Press them further into the mortar if necessary. Spray lightly with water if the mix is too dry, and clean any mortar off the stones.

Right: *Mixing materials breaks up a large area of the garden and prevents it from looking dull.*

Boundaries

Hedges, fences and walls are often overlooked at the garden-planning stage. It is tempting to see them simply as boundary markers within which the garden proper is arranged. Often it is only when the garden is complete and the boundary lowers the standard of the whole garden, that its importance is realized. A rotting fence or an ugly and overgrown hedge will mar the garden it borders, and it is much easier to consider the boundary at the design stage than it is to modify it when construction is complete.

Low walls are very practical as boundaries, and generally require much less maintenance than fences and hedges, but they often fail visually because they are too low to support most climbers and wall shrubs. Walls with a planting cavity at the top offer scope for color and interest, but the photograph on the opposite page (below) shows how planting can be taken a step farther by providing a planting trough towards the bottom.

If you don't want to go to the trouble and expense of making a tiered wall, a similar effect can be achieved by planting slightly taller plants directly into the ground. Bear in mind, however, that plants used within the wall or at the bottom must receive regular watering. The soil at the bottom of a wall is often much drier than it is some distance away because of the rain shadow effect.

Fences, too, make good boundaries but some are more elegant than others. If well maintained, white-painted picket is one of the most attractive. This is not the first choice if privacy and security is required – when a more practical but less appealing closeboard or solid panel fence might be a better option – but in a setting with plenty of greenery and the protection of shrubs beyond the garden, it can be ideal.

Traditionally, picket fences are made from wood, but there are plastic versions if you prefer a wipe-down finish.

Many flowering shrubs can be clipped into hedges, though pruning must be done with care to avoid cutting away next year's flowers. They are also best left informal rather than clipped too rigidly. This is Spiraea x arguta.

If you have a functional but unattractive boundary fence or wall, you can hide it with shrubs, which then become the effective boundary from the visual viewpoint. In a small garden like this one, the skill lies in choosing shrubs that will grow to the height of the true boundary to mask it, without growing much larger – otherwise they can appear oppressive. Most shrubs tolerate regular pruning to keep them within bounds, however, so height and spread can usually be controlled by regular use of the pruners.

In this town garden, the boundary has, in effect, become the garden – and what lies within it is the "human area," which is cosily protected as well as stylish in appearance.

Left: *A planting trough has been added to this low wall on the road side so that passers-by derive most of the pleasure, but the same technique can be used on the garden side, too.*

Above: *The use of white-painted garden furniture with a white picket fence helps to make a garden look more serene, designed and coordinated.*

Beating the Hedge

Hedges can be a chore. They are dusty and tiring to cut, and too frequently they are a trifle boring and over-large into the bargain.

Lifting and replanting a hedge is a big job, but there's a lot you can do to make lighter work of it once it is established. Buying a suitable electric trimmer of appropriate size, reducing the surface area to be cut, and even using a growth retardant, will all make life easier.

If you're feeling energetic and planning for the future, you might want to consider replanting with an attractive flowering or foliage hedge that might provide less of a barrier but will look brighter and won't demand maintenance or clipping so often.

Right: *You can sometimes improve the shape of a straight-sided hedge by sloping the sides, which will also marginally reduce the amount of hedge to be cut. Sloping sides can better withstand a heavy snowfall and allow more light to reach to the base of the hedge on each side.*

Very wide hedges can sometimes be reduced in width, but if it's a boundary hedge you should talk to your neighbor first. The best way to reduce the width is to insert painted canes – to make them easier to see – 1 ft further in than you want the final edge to be, to allow for new growth.

Cut back to the markers. If the stems are thick and tough, you may need a saw or long-handled pruners instead of hand pruners. This is best done in winter or early spring for deciduous hedges, and in late spring for evergreens. A year later, trim the new growth back to the desired width.

Left: *A low height and tapering sides will make cutting easier and quicker.*

CHEMICAL PRUNING

If you have a formal, clipped quick-growing hedge that you want to keep looking well without having to trim too often, look for a growth regulator sold for the purpose. These are sprayed onto the hedge after trimming, to inhibit further growth of the leading shoots. A few long shoots may grow out from within the hedge, but are easily trimmed off. You can spray your side of the hedge without affecting growth on your neighbor's side.

Not all hedges are suitable for this treatment, and they must be over three years old. You must spray on a calm day to avoid spray drift. Read the manufacturer's instructions carefully, and bear in mind the cost and time involved in spraying.

Right: *You may be able to save time on hedge-trimming by reducing the area to be cut. If your hedge is 6 ft tall and 2 ft across, reducing the height to 4 ft will reduce the amount of hedge to be cut by around 30 per cent. This saving alone is significant, but the top of a 4 ft hedge is also easier to cut than one 2 ft higher, for which you may need steps.*

Many established hedges will respond to quite severe height reduction. But remember that you should cut back to about 1 ft lower than you want the final height, to allow for new growth.

LONG BLADE, SHORT TRIM

A powered hedge trimmer is essential if you want to cut down on the time and effort involved in clipping hedges. If the hedge is very small, consider a trimmer that operates from a rechargeable battery rather than struggle on with hand shears.

For a large hedge, think about blade length. A 2 ft blade will knock a third off the cutting time in comparison with a 16 in blade. However, a longer blade means more weight and the trimmer will probably be more tiring to use, so you may prefer a blade length between the two as a compromise.

Clothing the Garden Walls

Climbers that need regular pruning, training or tying are best avoided, no matter how beautiful they may be. There are plenty of others that will clothe a wall with the minimum of attention. If you like more demanding plants like clematis and roses, try growing them the natural way – through other shrubs.

PLANTING A CLIMBER

Climbers need special care when planted in the dry soil near a wall or fence.

1 The soil close to walls and fences, or other shrubs and trees, is usually dry because of the "rain shadow" created. Always make the planting hole at least 1½ ft away, and work plenty of moisture-holding material such as garden compost or manure into the soil.

2 Plant at an angle so that the stems grow towards the wall. Leave in any cane that was used as a support while in the pot, but if there are several stems untie them and spread them out a little.

3 Self-clinging plants will not require a trellis and will cling without help. But to start it off when newly planted, use small ties that you can fix to the wall by suction or a special adhesive.

4 Water thoroughly, not only after planting but whenever the ground is dry for the first season. The roots can usually find moisture once well established, but are vulnerable initially.

Right: *Some climbers like this* Clematis montana *var.* rubens, *can be trained over thick ropes to produce a garland effect.*

Left: *Some climbers such as clematis and roses can be allowed to grow naturally through another shrub or into a tree. You can even let these two plants grow through each other.*

Screens and Disguises

Unless you are extremely fortunate, there will be a view or objects within the garden that you want to hide. Focal points can be used to take the eye away from some of them, but others will require some form of screening or disguise.

Many common hedging plants can be allowed to grow taller than normal to form a shrubby screen. Space the plants farther apart than for a hedge, so that they retain a shrubby shape, and clip or prune only when it is necessary to keep within bounds. Avoid a formal, clipped shape unless you are screening within a very formal garden. Most hedging plants will grow to twice their normal hedge height if you give them more space and do not restrict them by frequent clipping and pruning.

Choose plants appropriate to the setting. In a Japanese-style garden, many of the tall bamboos will make an excellent screen for, say, a garage wall or oil storage tank. Use shrubby plants in a garden where there are lots of shrubs, and especially if the shrub border can be taken up to the screening point. On a patio, a climber-covered trellis may look more appropriate.

In town gardens, and especially in the case of balcony and roof gardens, the problem is to minimize the impact of surrounding homes, offices and factories. These usually require impracticably huge walls to mask the view, which would also make the garden excessively dark. In a very small garden, trees may not be a practical solution for this type of screening either, although in a large one they will probably provide the answer.

A sensible compromise is to extend the wall or fence with a trellis, or similar framework, along which you can grow climbers. This will not block out the view completely, but it will soften the harsh impact of buildings and help to concentrate the eye within the garden by minimizing the distractions beyond. The boundary itself will be given extra height and interest.

A combination of plants and hard landscaping is often the most pleasing way to screen a view beyond a boundary. Trees are a particularly pleasing solution. Even if they lose their leaves in winter, the network of branches is often sufficient to break up the harsh outline of buildings beyond, and in summer – when you are in the garden and require more privacy – the canopy of foliage will usually block out most of the view beyond. Trees are a particularly good solution if the aspect is such that most of the shadow falls away from your garden rather than over it.

A painted trellis makes an attractive and easily erected screen, and if you make it tall enough and use it to form an L-shaped corner where you can create a cosy sitting area, the screen can become an attractive feature in its own right. The secret of stylish screening is to turn it into a positive feature whenever possible. If you give it a purpose, it will be less obviously a screen intended to hide something and become a positive part of your garden.

Left: *Using bright flowers or interesting focal points within a garden concentrates the eye on the positive points and not the negative surrounding ones.*

Above: *In this garden, an arbor has been created that provides height and privacy, with climbers over the top adding even more screening.*

The strong formal design, with a circle at its center, also uses a design technique that takes the eye inward rather than outward to what lies beyond the boundary. This clever use of clay pavers shows a circular centerpiece laid to an angled herringbone pattern, with basket-weave used for the rectangular areas of paving.

Changing the View

The French call it *trompe l'oeil*, and deceiving the eye is an illusion a garden designer often has to adopt to make the most of an unpromising site. The few simple forms of visual deception described here should enable you to make your garden look larger than it really is or help to distract the eye from the unappealing features by making the most of the positive.

Straight lines can be uncompromising, and a dominant feature at the end of a straight path will foreshorten the visual appearance. By curving the path slightly, and perhaps tapering it slightly toward the end, there will be the illusion of greater depth. If the focal point is also diminished in height or stature, the optical illusion will be increased.

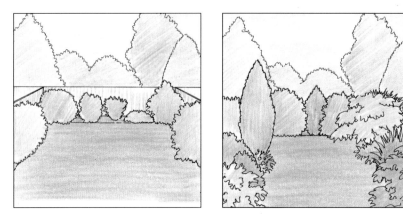

If the boundary is clearly visible, and especially if plain and man-made like a fence or a wall, a small garden will seem box-like and the boundary will dominate. Simply adding a narrow border with masking shrubs will not help because the boundary, although better clothed, will still be obvious.

By bringing the border into the garden in broad sweeps, with a hint of the lawn disappearing behind a sweep toward the end of the garden, the boundaries will be blurred and there will be the illusion of more garden beyond.

A long, straight path will take the eye to the boundary unless the garden is very large, so try to introduce a feature that will arrest the eye part way along the path. A curve around an ornament, a large shrub or small tree, will keep the eye within the garden. If you do not want to move an existing path, try erecting an arch over it, with an attractive climber to soften the outline and perhaps extended along a length of trellis on either side.

Right: *Apart from their obvious role, some colors have the visual effect of making things seem nearer or more distant, dominant or receding. This yellow* Acer japonicum *"Aureum" brings the eye to rest within the garden rather than at the garden wall or beyond. In turn, it takes the eye to the attractive stone table that might otherwise go unnoticed from a distance as its tones blend so well with the background.*

If your garden is small, and your neighbor's is attractive, leave a space between the borders and bridge the gap with an inconspicuous type of fence. The eye will then go beyond the fence, especially if there is a bold plant or tree in the distance, and create the illusion that your own garden extends much farther than it actually does.

Mirrors can be used to create great illusions, and can be invaluable in making a small area look larger than it really is. A mirror placed in the frame of a disused gate – or in a false frame – will give the illusion that there is more garden beyond the door or gateway.

The combination of mirror and water, one reflected in the other, can have a dramatic effect, as this photograph shows.

Consult a mirror supplier before installing one in your garden, and explain what it is required for. You should be able to have one made to the required size if you measure carefully first.

The illusion is soon shattered if you let the glass become dirty, so be prepared to keep the mirror really clean.

GARDEN FEATURES

Focal Points

Focal points are an essential part of good garden design, relevant whatever the size of garden. They help to take the eye to a favorable part and away from the less favorable, and can act as signposts to lead the eye around the garden.

Even a well-kept lawn will look bare and a little boring if it's large and all the interest is in beds and borders around the edges. It can be useful to create a focal point within the lawn, but this often works better if offset to one side or toward the end of the lawn, rather than in the center. Position it where you want to take the eye to an attractive view, or use it to fill an area that lacks interest. Try to avoid placing the focal point against a background that is already interesting or colorful; otherwise one will fight with the other for attention.

A sundial is a popular choice, but is best placed in a sunny position if it is to look in the least credible. A birdbath is another popular choice, especially if it is close to the house where the birds can be seen and enjoyed.

Above: *Gateways and arches make excellent focal points, and if used to divide a large garden, can add a sense of mystery and promise from whichever side you view. This device works best if the areas either side are in contrasting styles or are visually very different. The garden on one side of this wall is heavily planted and enclosed, whereas the view beyond suggests open lawns and spaciousness.*

In a long, narrow garden, you could produce a series of arches or gates, each taking the eye farther on into a journey of exploration.

Left: *Focal points can be plants as well as inanimate objects. When the two are used together, the effect can be particularly striking.*

In this garden, the mature hedges produce a predominantly green effect: restful but visually uninspiring. A statue has transformed an unexciting view into an arresting scene that demands attention. But foreground plants are important too and, if large, can help to put the rest of the garden into more reasonable proportions. These bold red-hot pokers (Kniphofia) have the height to counterbalance the statue, and their strong color accentuates the effect.

In a small garden it can be a good idea to have the sitting area away from the house so that there appears to be a larger area of interest between home and boundary. In this attractive scene, the white chairs provide the necessary contrast and height to act as a focal point. This only works well, however, if the background is attractive – avoid taking the eye toward a sagging old fence.

A tall, narrow object such as a birdbath or sundial on a plinth needs added visual impact from a distance, and setting it on a bold base like this graveled area edged with bricks is one way to achieve this.

In a small garden, a spectacular focal point can be used to dominate a corner of the garden so that the limitations of scale and size become irrelevant for the moment. A well-placed ornament or figure will serve as a simple focal point. In this garden, the white trellis that frames the statue helps to fill this particular corner, and immediately creates the impression of style and elegance.

Using Furniture

A garden without furniture implies a garden that is all work and no play. Furniture creates the impression of a garden designed to be used for relaxation, a place to rest and enjoy the fruit of earlier labors. It has to be used with care, however, as the choice of material and the style of furniture can look incongruous if it does not reflect the mood of the rest of the garden. Some furniture is purely functional, while other pieces can be as important a focal point as a well-chosen ornament.

Furniture can become the feature of a paved area, especially if it lacks a natural focal point. Although the garden featured on the right immediately generates a pleasant atmosphere, any clear-cut lines that relate to an overall plan are obscured by the difficult site. In an area heavily shaded by trees, the paving gives the illusion of an area in a forest clearing, with dappled light filtering through. Without the containers and the furniture, this kind of area could lack visual stimulation and look rather barren. The lavish use of plants in containers gives it color and texture, but it is the furniture that draws the eye and holds the area together.

Tree seats have a special charm, and are often useful as a focal point in a part of the garden otherwise lacking interest, such as areas of grass with large trees and little else. If painted white, a tree seat will stand out across the garden, and is sure to add a touch of elegance.

Tree seats are more useful as a focal point and garden ornament than as practical seats, however, as the white paint soon looks grubby and unpleasant unless you wipe it off regularly, and drips, insects and falling leaves are always a risk if you sit beneath the overhanging branches of a tree.

In this setting, white plastic or resin furniture would sit uneasily, but wood blends with the paving and the woodland effect of the setting. Cushions – which must be taken inside when not in use – add another dash of restrained color, and will help to offset the rather austere appearance that some wooden furniture often has.

Use an attractive garden seat to liven up an otherwise dull area of the garden, perhaps where mainly green shrubs or a dark hedge forms a backdrop to the lawn. As these photographs show, a scene that is rather mundane and uninteresting can be transformed by the simple addition of a garden seat. It also invites you to walk over to it, and to use a part of the garden that may not otherwise hold special appeal.

BUILT-IN FURNITURE

Built-in furniture is a sensible option for a patio where space is limited. If you have plenty of space, freestanding furniture is much more adaptable, and by rearranging it you can add variety. In a small area, however, built-in seats and a barbecue can give your patio a very "designed" appearance. You will still require supplementary freestanding furniture of course, but less of it.

Barbecues and wooden seats are commonly integrated into the walls created as part of the patio boundary, but if you have a raised bed around the edge, a simple sitting area like the one illustrated below will give that special feeling that you get when surrounded by plants. Bear in mind, of course, that when certain plants are in flower, like this geranium, bees and wasps may be a problem.

Above: *Tree seats almost always have to be made to measure and adapted to suit the diameter of the tree – or in this case the area occupied by multiple trunks – which gives great scope for that touch of individuality in design.*

Left: *Built-in seats can be very straightforward to create, like this concrete "seat."*

Water Features

Water plays an important part in most good garden design, and if you look at the work of many professional garden designers you will find water somewhere. Not everyone wants a pond, of course, especially if safety is a concern where there are young children, but there are lots of water features where the risk is minimal while still creating maximum impact as a focal point. Whether or not you include a pond, try to find space for a simple water feature such as a wall or pebble fountain.

Wall fountains are a good choice for a formal garden or a patio, although they can also be used with great effect in an informal setting too. Lion faces and gargoyles look perfectly in place in a period garden.

You can buy suitable wall masks complete as a kit with pump. If you don't want a small pool at the bottom like the one in the photograph on the opposite page, buy an integrated wall fountain that includes a shallow dish that fixes to the wall along with the spout. This can be positioned beyond the reach of small children, and in any case the basins contain very little water.

Only a small pump is required, and these can be powered by a simple low-voltage system.

A wall fountain is usually fitted by drilling and plugging the wall, so that it can be screwed into position. The difficult part is disguising the pipe between the submerged pump and the wall spout. The pipe is best hidden within the brickwork when the wall is constructed, but often this is not possible. You may be able to remove a channel in the brickwork, but the pipework will still be visible unless you camouflage it. The simplest way to fix the pipe to an existing wall is to clamp it to the face of the brick and then plant ivy or some other evergreen climber to cover it. After a year or two, the pipe probably will not be visible from a distance.

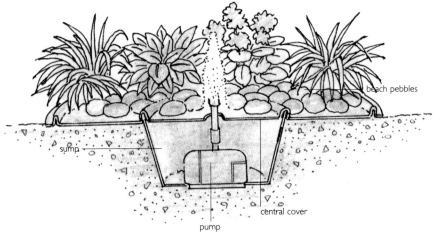

Above: *Simple fountains like this can be bought complete with reservoir and pump. Making this pebble fountain can take just one day.*

MAKING A PEBBLE POOL

1 For any bubble fountain or pebble pool you will need a reservoir, or sump, to house the pump and hold a generous reserve of water. Commercial products are by far the easiest to install as they are designed with a wide rim to catch water that has drifted, with a centerpiece to support the pebbles over the reservoir. Most garden centers stock these, or you can order them from water garden specialists.

   Make sure the reservoir is well supported, removing or adding more soil as necessary. If the soil is very stony, bed on a layer of sand. Make sure it is level, with the rim at or just below the surrounding paving or soil. If surrounded by soil, positioning the lip slightly above bed level will reduce the amount of soil contaminating the fountain.

2 Insert the pump and take the wire out at a side where it can be hidden easily as it emerges from the wide rim. If there is paving on one side and a flowerbed on the other, take it out on the flowerbed side so that it can easily be camouflaged.

3 Insert the central cover, then add the pebbles. You can buy these from some garden centers; otherwise obtain them from a builder's merchant or collect them at the shore.

4 Fill with water and turn on the pump. Installing a spectacular water feature like this is that simple.

Above: *It is always a good idea to have plenty of plants growing around a wall fountain; otherwise attention will drawn to what could be an expanse of plain brickwork.*

Right: *Rock gardens and streams with cascades are a natural choice for a sloping site, and they can often be combined. If the slope is gentle, the design could be mainly lawn with rock and water features as the main theme of the garden.*

Left: *Simple but effective water features can be built for little cost. This one has been made from an old garbage can lid! The lid is supported over a reservoir that also contains a small low-voltage pump, and shingle has been used to give the feature more interest and character. The water simply flows over the rim and into the reservoir to be recirculated.*

The reservoir can be made from the bottom of a cut-down garbage can, or a waterproof container (you can even just use an excavation in the ground and line it with a waterproof pond liner). Some water is lost regularly through evaporation and splashes that drift in the wind. So if you cannot see the water level in the reservoir, make a point of topping it up every few days (simply pour more water into the basin or over the stones – if the reservoir is full, it will overflow into the surrounding ground).

Creating a Pond

Overcrowded plants benefit from division and replanting in spring, and in the fall it's best to cut down dead foliage that might pollute the water, and to rake out most of the leaves that fall in. Apart from that, however, ponds are very low on maintenance. They don't require cleaning out annually, although it is worth giving them a cleaning every second spring.

MAKING A LINED POOL

You can make this in a weekend. The only hard part is excavating the hole.

1 Make your pool as large as possible – it will make a better feature, the fish and wildlife will be happier, and the water will probably stay clearer. Start by marking out the shape with a garden hose or rope.

PLANTS FOR PONDS

Iris laevigata (Japanese iris)
Pontederia cordata (Pickerel weed)
Azolla caroliniana (mosquito plant)
Aponegeton distachysos
(Cape pondweed)
Acorus graminens 'Variegatus'
(grassy-leaved sweet flag)
Juncus effusus 'Spiralis'
(Corkscrew rush)
Myriophyllum aquaticum
(parrot's feather)

2 Excavate the soil to the required depth, but leave a shallow ledge about 9 in down around part of the pond. This is for plants that require shallow water. If you are having a paved edge, remove enough grass for this, remembering to allow for the mortar bed as well as the thickness of the paving. It is essential to check the levels all round. Use a carpenter's level in all directions.

3 Remove any sharp stones or large roots, then line the pool with a ½ in layer of sand (it will stick to the sides if damp). If the soil is very stony, use a polyester mat (sold by water garden suppliers) instead of sand.

4 Drape the liner loosely over the excavation, with an overlap all round. Hold the edges in place with a few bricks, then fill with a garden hose.

5 As the weight of the water takes the liner into the pool, lift the bricks periodically to allow the liner to mold easily into the excavation. Try to remove some of the worst creases as the water fills, but don't expect to be able to eliminate all of them.

6 Once the water has reached its final height, trim off the surplus liner, leaving a 6 in overlap all round. Lay the paving on a bed of mortar, trapping the edge of the liner. Make sure the paving overlaps the edge by an inch or two, so that any drop in water level is not so noticeable.

PLANTING A POND

The best time to plant aquatics is spring and early summer.

1 Use a planting basket designed for aquatic plants, and line it with a special basket liner made for the purpose (or use a piece of horticultural fleece cut to size). Plant in garden soil or an aquatic soil. Do not use a potting soil intended for ordinary pots as this will contain too much fertilizer.

2 Cover the surface with gravel. This will reduce the chance of the water becoming muddied when placing the basket in the pond, and should also deter fish from stirring up the soil.

3 Most waterlilies should be planted in deeper water, but miniature waterlilies and all the "marginal" plants should be placed on the planting shelf at the edge.

Above: *A raised patio pool like this makes an eye-catching feature for a small garden. You can also use a liner to waterproof this kind of pool.*

Lighting

Enjoyment of your garden should not cease at sundown. Garden lighting will enable you to sit outside on warm evenings when you can see your garden in a new light, and in the cold dark days of winter you can enjoy spectacular effects from indoors.

Do not be afraid to try garden lighting just because electricity is potentially dangerous. There are lots of excellent systems that should remove the worry, and for mains voltage consult your local qualified electrician for assistance.

In small town gardens, roof gardens and on balconies, floodlights and spotlights of the kind that can be so effective in a large garden may be inappropriate. Glaring lights may annoy neighbors, so more subtle lighting is usually more suitable. Small lanterns, and low-voltage lamps that cast their beam downwards or over just a small area, are unlikely to offend anyone. The use of some stronger patio lighting will be necessary, however, for an area that you are going to use in the evening. Just make sure most of the beam is focused towards the ground, which is where it is needed for safety.

For lighting to be a permanent feature, electric lighting is the practical option, but candles and flares can be used for the odd occasion when you want to invite your friends around for an evening out with a difference, a true candlelight dinner perhaps. Patio flares burn quite brightly, and lanterns are available that will protect candles from the wind and cast a reasonably localized light. Candles are for "atmospheric" light, however, and are really only practical where there is some supplementary light from a nearby electric lamp, from the house for instance.

Garden lighting can also be used to create focal points after dark, but the spotlights for this are best installed during construction to avoid the problem of laying cables across or around paved and heavily planted areas. Ideally, several lighting points should be wired in at this stage, giving you plenty of flexibility later so that the lights can be moved around to make the most of seasonal variations.

Spotlights should be unobtrusive by day – preferably well hidden among some plants. Upward-pointing beams can be very striking and effective, but it is best to avoid them if the beams are likely to be thrown into your neighbors' windows.

INSTALLING GARDEN LIGHTING

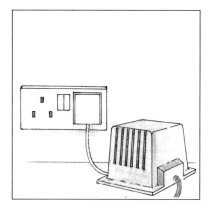

1 Garden lighting is simple to install, and usually comes in a kit with everything you need.

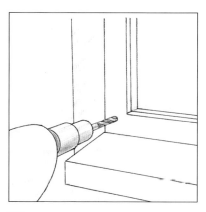

2 Drill a hole in the wall or window frame to pass the cable through. Fill the hole with caulk to produce a waterproof seal around the cable.

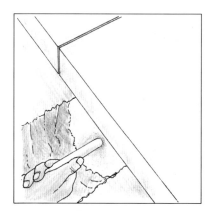

3 Whenever possible, take the cable underground. Electrically, it is not a hazard to life because of the low voltage it carries, but trailing cables are a hazard as you may trip over them. Paths are a special problem, and the cable should be passed under them whenever possible. Excavate an area on either side, undercutting the path a little, and then push through a piece of conduit. Thread the cable through the conduit.

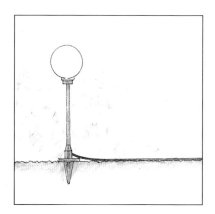

4 You should have a choice of designs for the lights, so choose those that are appropriate to the style of the garden and their position. A kit usually includes several lights, which are easy to fix and reposition if you follow the manufacturer's instructions.

Spotlights are often used to pick out ornaments or striking structural features, but bold plants such as red hot pokers (Kniphofia) and yuccas make good focal points at night. In this picture fennel takes center stage.

In this beautiful garden, the decorative lighting has been confined to chains of small lights draped through the tree, and to a small lantern. Light from the house, or supplementary lighting, is turned on when the area is used for sitting out in the evening during the summer.

Flares and candlelight contribute enormously to the atmosphere when you are relaxing outside in the evening.

Creating Planting Schemes

Structural features such as paving and walls may give a garden a strong sense of design, but it is the soft furnishings – the plants – which fill out the skeleton with shape and texture. Whether you are looking for a traditional, formal look, or something more out of the ordinary or easy to maintain, strikingly diverse effects can be achieved within the same design framework by using different planting schemes.

Left: *Some of the best displays are improvised – here, an expanse of gravel has been broken up by a vibrant border which has been planted through it.*

Above: *A single-sided mixed border is a classic choice for the garden and will provide color for many months of the year.*

Going Wild

Most of us like to coax certain wildlife into the garden. You can encourage wildlife simply by feeding the birds, making a pond, and growing plants that butterflies are attracted to. A true wildlife enthusiast will want to go one step farther, however, and design the garden with wildlife in mind. Whether this kind of gardening appeals or not depends on whether you can look at buttercups and daisies and see them as attractive wild flowers, or only as weeds.

A more acceptable compromise for many are normal flower borders given over mainly to wild flowers. Here various poppies and forget-me-nots have self-seeded to provide an undisturbed wild area that is visually attractive and easily managed. Some weeding may be necessary to prevent particularly rampant weeds taking over the bed or border, but generally a bed like this will look after itself.

It is worth clearing the area of weeds first, leaving it for weed seedlings to germinate before weeding again, then sowing a wild flower seed mixture. In this way you are more likely to have a bed with a good range of attractive wild flowers rather than the dominant local weeds.

A wildlife pond usually looks rather overgrown, but that's how it should be. Wildlife is less attracted to large areas of clear water with fountains and cascades than to areas of still water almost congested with plant growth.

It is also important to have some shelter close to the pond, such as a border, an area with bog plants, or even a hedge. Wildlife is much more vulnerable in an open position, but choose a bright position rather than one in dense shade.

Although shape is relatively unimportant, some shallow beach edges are crucial, so that amphibians and other creatures can gain access to the water easily, and climb out without difficulty. An area of shallow water will also encourage birds and other animals to use the pond for drinking.

Whether you could live with this as part of your back lawn depends on the relative appeal of gardening against wildlife. If you like a neat and tidy garden with lots of flowerbeds, this kind of wildlife feature will not appeal. But even a small area of long grass like this will encourage a wide range of birds (especially when seeds ripen), insects and mammals. You should also be able to introduce many attractive wild flowers into an area like this, and of course there is less grass to mow!

Many common garden plants will attract butterflies, especially Buddleia davidii, *the butterfly-bush. Other common flowers attract butterflies too: this is a small tortoiseshell on a hyacinth.*

Left: *With a wild garden, you need only cut the long grass areas once or twice a year, and let nature do the rest. If there are rare flowers among the buttercups and daisies, you will have to time any cutting carefully to avoid interfering with their natural growth cycles; some parts can be left completely uncultivated. This will attract a wide range of wildlife, most of which will venture into the more ornamental part of the garden as well.*

Flowers that Sow Themselves

Plants that germinate readily from self-sown seeds can be a problem in the wrong place, but you can use them freely in areas that have a natural boundary, such as a bed in a lawn, or around a tree or shrub. You will, of course, have to sow them initially.

Right: *These* Aquilegia alpinum *have sown themselves, and all the gardener had to do was a little thinning and weeding in the spring.*

HOW TO START THEM OFF

Decide on a position where the plants can multiply freely without becoming a nuisance. Suitable places are among shrubs and herbaceous plants, especially in a mixed bed, or in beds restrained by clear boundaries. Don't sow them where you will have to keep weeding out the seedlings where they're not wanted.

SELF-SOWING ANNUALS

Calendula (pot marigold)
Eschscholtzia (Californian poppies)
Limnanthes (poached egg plant)
Linaria (toad flax)

SELF-SOWING PERENNIALS

Aquilegia (columbine)
Lupinus (lupine)
Foeniculum vulgare (fennel)
Digitalis (foxglove) (a biennial)

1 Start with weed-free ground. Hoe off or pull out any weeds in the area you want to sow. Fork out any deep-rooted perennial weeds.

2 Annuals used for this purpose are best scattered randomly rather than sown in rows. Avoid sowing too thickly otherwise you'll have more thinning to do.

3 Perennials, like lupines and columbines, should be sown in small pinches about 18 in apart, instead of being scattered randomly.

4 Simply rake the annual seeds in, first in one direction and then the other if possible. Pull some soil over the perennials sown in spaced pinches. Keep watered until they germinate and are growing well.

5 After initial sowing, and each subsequent year, pull out any weed seedlings before they compete with the sown seedlings. You should be able to identify the desirable seedlings by the larger number with the same kind of leaf.

6 As the seedlings become larger, hoe between them to control weeds. Once the plants meet, you should be able to stop weeding.

Easy Bedding

If you like the cheerful brightness of seasonal bedding rather than the permanent but predictable show from shrubs and border plants, you can compromise by using a mixture of seasonal and permanent plants. This will reduce the amount of regular replanting and save on cost as well as time.

If you do want to use traditional summer bedding plants, choose those that flower prolifically over a long period without deadheading. Some of the most trouble-free and spectacular bedding plants to use are suggested opposite.

PLANTING A PERMANENT EDGING

Perennials will form the basis of the edging, with bedding plants added for variety.

1 Always dig over the ground and clear it of weeds before planting.

2 Rake in a general fertilizer before planting. (Wait until spring to apply the fertilizer if planting in fall or winter.) This will encourage vigorous early growth and help the plants to knit together more quickly.

BE ECONOMICAL WITH THE ANNUALS

These pictures show how imaginatively you can use summer bedding plants in combination with perennials. The plants you choose should reflect your own preferences, but the concept is easy to adapt to your own needs.

3 Space out the plants in their pots first, in case you have to adjust them to go evenly around the bed.

4 Plant with a trowel, adjusting the spacing to suit the plant. About 6 in apart is suitable for most plants if you want quick cover, further apart if you don't mind waiting a little longer for a carpeting effect.

5 Firm in to remove large pockets of air, then water thoroughly. Keep well watered for the first few weeks. The bed may be planted immediately with spring or summer bedding plants or bulbs as appropriate. When they have finished, lift them but leave the perennial edging.

Begonia 'White Devil'

Impatiens (busy lizzie)

Left: Impatiens *(busy lizzie) and begonias are popular choices for colorful beds.*

NO-FUSS SUMMER BEDDING PLANTS

The following will continue to flower for many months without deadheading, regular attention or watering.

Begonia semperflorens
Impatiens (busy lizzie)
Lavatera trimestris
Osteospermums
Pelargoniums (bedding geraniums)
Petunias
Tagetes patula (French marigolds)

Right: *This edging is the perennial* Sedum spurium *'Album Superbum', but many other carpeting plants can be used (beware of very invasive sedums, however). This provides a neat year-round edging that you don't have to replace and at most needs an annual trim to keep it neat. Fill the center of the bed with spring and summer bedding plants.*

Self-sufficient Shrubs

Some of the most popular shrubs – like roses and buddleias – need a lot of attention if they are to remain looking good. Pruning is a regular requirement for many of them, and those prone to pests and diseases are bad news unless you are prepared to spend time spraying or dusting too. But for every shrub that is a potential problem for the low-maintenance gardener, there are many more that are just as attractive and almost totally trouble-free.

There are hundreds of well-behaved compact shrubs that will not demand frequent pruning or hacking back. If in doubt, check with your garden center to make sure the shrubs you choose don't need regular pruning, won't become bare and leggy at the base with all the flowers at the top, and aren't susceptible to diseases.

PLANTING SHRUBS

Shrubs will be in position for many years, so take your time over planting and prepare the ground thoroughly.

1 Water the pots thoroughly and let them drain, then position them where you think they should be in the border. Check the likely size on the label or in a book, then revise your spacing if necessary. If the spacing seems excessive initially, you can always plant a few extra inexpensive shrubs between them to discard when they become overcrowded.

2 Fork over the area, and remove any weeds. Then fork in as much rotted manure or garden compost as you can spare, or use a commercial planting mix.

3 Excavate a hole large enough to take the rootball. Stand the pot in the hole and use a cane or stick to check that the plant will be at its original depth in the soil when planted. Add or remove soil as necessary.

4 Carefully tease out some of the roots if they are tightly wound around the inside of the pot. This will encourage them to grow out into the surrounding soil more quickly.

5 Return the soil and firm it well around the roots to steady the shrub in wind and to prevent large pockets of air that might allow the roots to dry out. Pressing the earth in with your heel is the most effective way of firming the soil around a shrub.

6 Apply a balanced fertilizer according to the manufacturer's instructions, if planting in spring or summer. Hoe or rake it into the surface, then water thoroughly.

Right: *A border like this is planted with* Choisya ternata *'Sundance' a low-maintenance shrub, and Michaelmas daisies, and remains bright and beautiful for many months of the year.*

SELF-SUFFICIENT FLOWERING SHRUBS

Cistus
Escallonia
Hibiscus syriacus
Hypericum
Mahonia
Olearia × *haastii*
Yucca

SELF-SUFFICIENT FOLIAGE SHRUBS

Aucuba japonica
Berberis thunbergii
Choisya ternata
Elaeagnus pungens 'Maculata'
Euonymus fortunei
Ruscus aculeatus
Viburnum davidii

Make the Most of Trees

Trees largely look after themselves, and make attractive features as specimens set in a lawn, or planted towards the back of a shrub border.

Trees in a border are generally less trouble because falling leaves drop almost unnoticed onto the soil and are quickly recycled. Leaves on a lawn usually have to be raked up, and mowing beneath a low-hanging tree or up to a trunk can also cause difficulties. Don't be deterred from trying a tree in a lawn, but choose one with small or evergreen leaves, and try some of the tips suggested below to make mowing and cultivating around the base easier.

TREES IN LAWNS

Mowing will be frustratingly difficult if you take the grass right up to the trunk of the tree, especially as it becomes larger. Lawn trees are generally better planted in a bed cut into the grass, which you can plant with some of the ground cover plants suggested for borders, or cover with a decorative mulch to suppress weeds.

TREES IN BORDERS

The best way to cover the ground beneath trees in a border is with ground cover plants that will tolerate shade and dry soil. If the tree is very large, or has large leaves, you may have to rake them off the plants when they fall, but most of them usually work their way between the plants and soon rot down. If you use a ground cover that dies down in winter, falling leaves will not matter.

HOW TO PLANT A LAWN TREE

Trees often look best planted in isolation in a lawn.

1 With sand, mark a circle on the grass about 3–4 ft across. Lift the grass with a spade, and remove about 6 in of soil with it. Fork in as much garden compost or manure as possible.

2 Insert a short stake before you plant, placing it on the side of the prevailing wind. Place it off-center, to allow space for the rootball. A short stake is preferable to a long one.

3 If planting a bare-root tree, spread out the roots. Place the tree in the hole and use a cane to check that the soil mark on the tree's stem will be at final soil level, about 2 in below the grass.

4 Return the soil, and firm in well. Water thoroughly and secure with a tree tie. Use a thick ornamental organic mulch to suppress weeds and make the bed look more attractive.

Right: *Once established* Hedera colchica *'Dentata-variegata' will form an attractive evergreen carpet that will suppress weeds and needs practically no attention.*

Left: *Use beach pebbles instead of an organic mulch to make an attractive feature. They will prevent weed growth and can look very ornamental.*

A RAISED EDGE

Raising the edge makes more of a feature of the bed, but you won't easily be able to mow up to the edge unless you also make a mowing strip. A sunken border about 4–6 in wide all round will enable you to mow over the edge without striking the raised edge.

Using Grasses

A grass lawn can be high maintenance, but a grass bed can make a striking feature that will not take up much of your time. Grasses can also be used in mixed beds and borders, but be careful as some of them will make a take-over bid for territory and can be difficult to eradicate if entwined with other border plants. Choose well-behaved clump-forming species or plant in a container as shown below.

PLANTING GRASSES

Groups of grasses are refreshingly different, but beware of the rampant species.

3 Firm the soil around the roots, using your hand or heel, then water in thoroughly. Keep watered in dry spells until the plants are well established.

4 If planting a spreading grass in a border, or even if using a rampant species in a grasses-only bed, plant it in a large pot or container to restrain its spread. This method is not suitable for very large grasses, but you are unlikely to be using these in a small border. Excavate a hole large enough to take the container, which must have drainage holes in it.

1 Grasses often work best as a low-maintenance feature in a bed of their own. There are many kinds to grow, from compact dwarfs for the edge to huge plants 8 ft or even taller. Study a specialist catalogue, and when you have bought the plants space them out to see how they will look.

2 Make sure the plants have been well watered beforehand, then knock out of the pot and plant in well-prepared, weed-free soil. If there are a lot of roots tightly wound around the edge of the pot, gently tease out some of them.

5 Partly fill the container with soil then plant normally, with the rootball at the correct level. Firm the plant well, and add more soil mix if necessary.

6 Make sure the rim is flush with the surrounding soil (but not below it, otherwise the most rampant grasses will escape), and for a more natural appearance make sure that the soil is flush with the rim. Water thoroughly.

Right: Grasses can be attractive plants to use in a border. Some can be used as an edging but most are used mid- or back-border.

Heathers

Heathers make excellent low-maintenance beds, with a guarantee of evergreen cover and – depending on the varieties used – colorful flowers practically the year round. Many have attractive golden foliage that looks good for twelve months of the year.

Use them with dwarf conifers if you want to add height, or alone for a carpet of living color. You could use them as a ground cover around the base of a birch tree with silver bark – winter-flowering varieties will look stunning.

Calluna vulgaris 'Blazeaway'

PLANTING A HEATHER BED
Prepare the soil thoroughly as some heathers have special needs. Although heathers will suppress weeds after they have been established for a couple of years or so, you will have to control weeds for the first few seasons.

1 Dig the soil thoroughly, and pull up as many deep-rooted or difficult perennial weeds as possible. Add plenty of organic material such as garden compost or rotted manure, especially if the soil is dry or impoverished.

2 If planting in spring or summer, rake in a balanced general fertilizer. If planting in fall or winter wait until spring to apply fertilizer.

Erica carnea

Above: *A combination of heathers, such as* Erica carnea *and* Calluna vulgaris*, will provide interesting color variations, even when not in flower.*

3 Some heathers, such as the winter-flowering *Erica carnea* varieties will grow on a neutral or even slightly alkaline soil. Many others, such as *Calluna vulgaris*, need an acid soil. Adding peat to the planting area will benefit all types.

4 Start planting at one end or at the back of the bed. Space the plants about 12–18 in apart, but the planting distance will vary with species and even variety, so check first.

5 Use a mulch to help suppress weeds, conserve moisture, and improve the appearance of the bare soil while the plants are still young. Peat is useful for this, but you may prefer to use a renewable alternative such as chipped bark.

Above: *Heathers make happy companions for conifers, and if you choose winter-flowering varieties like these* Erica carnea, *the garden will always be bright.*

PLANTING THROUGH PLASTIC
This method will cut down weeding to the absolute minimum.

1 Cover the whole area with black plastic or a plastic mulching sheet. Make cross-shaped slits in the plastic.

2 Plant through the slits in the sheet.

3 If you don't like the visual appearance of the plastic, cover it with a mulch of chipped bark.

Dwarf Conifers

Dwarf conifers need practically no attention after their first year, but to look effective they are best grown as a group with contrasting shapes, sizes and colors, or with colorful carpeters such as heathers.

PLANTING A CONIFER BED

A good garden center will have a bewildering array of dwarf and slow-growing conifers, but it is best to consult a good specialist catalogue or book before you buy. Some described as dwarf may reach 8 ft or so in time, and those described as slow-growing may be even larger eventually. Make sure your dwarf conifers really are dwarf if space is at a premium.

Chamaecyparis obtusa 'Aurea'

Chamaecyparis lawsonia 'Silver Threads'

Above: *These varieties are among many that need little care, but provide year-round color.*

1 Dwarf conifers look good in a small bed or border. If you find it difficult to plan beds and borders on paper, stand the pots where you think the plants will look good, and be prepared to shuffle them around until they look right. Bear in mind the eventual height and spread.

2 Dig a hole larger and deeper than the rootball. Stand the pot in the hole to make sure it is large enough.

3 Fork in as much rotted manure, garden compost, or planting mixture as you can spare. This is especially important on very dry soils, or near a fence or wall.

4 Add a controlled-release or slow-release fertilizer to the planting hole, using the manufacturer's recommended rate, and work in with a fork or trowel.

5 Make sure the soil in the pot is moist, then knock the plant out and check the roots. If they are very tightly wound around the inside of the pot, carefully tease some of them out so that they will grow into the surrounding soil.

6 Check the planting depth by standing the rootball in the hole, and using a cane or piece of wood to make sure it will be at its original depth when the soil is returned. Add or remove soil as necessary.

Right: *This bed shows how bright and colorful a conifer and heather bed can be, and it really is a low-maintenance combination.*

7 Firm in to eliminate large air pockets that might cause the roots to dry out, then water thoroughly.

8 Mulch with a decorative material such as chipped bark. Make sure the mulch is at least 2 in thick so that it will suppress weeds effectively.

Living Carpets

Ground cover is one of the labor-saving gardener's best weapons. It suppresses weeds, covers bare soil, and makes a really worthwhile visual contribution. Some of the flowering kinds of ground cover plants are both colorful and beautiful.

Right: Convallaria majalis *(lily-of-the-valley) takes a few years to become established, but then makes an effective as well as a fragrant ground cover.*

NON-WOODY GROUND COVERS

Ajuga reptans (E)
Alchemilla mollis
Anthemis nobilis (E)
Bergenia species (E)
Cerastium tomentosum (E)
Geranium endressii
Lamium maculatum
Pulmonaria species
Tiarella cordifolia (E)
Waldsteinia ternata (E)

(E) = evergreen

PLANTING GROUND COVER

Ground cover will eventually suppress weeds, but initially needs protection from them.

1 Clear the ground of weeds first. Annual weeds can be hoed off or killed with a herbicide. Some perennial weeds will have to be dug out by hand or killed by several applications of a translocated weedkiller, as regrowth occurs.

2 Fork in as much rotted manure or garden compost as you can spare, then apply a slow-release or controlled-release balanced fertilizer at the rate recommended by the manufacturer, and rake it in.

3 Unless planting a ground cover that spreads by underground stems or rooting prostrate stems on the surface, it is best to plant through a mulching sheet to control weeds while the plants are becoming established.

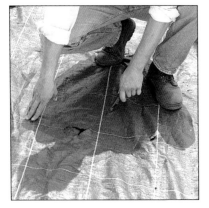

4 Spread out the mulching sheet. Using scissors or a sharp knife, cut a cross where the plant is to be positioned. Plant in staggered rows, at spacings appropriate for the plants.

5 Provided you use small plants, it should be easy to plant through the slits with a trowel. If using large ground-cover plants it may be better to omit the mulching sheet and plant with a spade.

6 Be sure to water thoroughly after planting, and in dry weather throughout the first year.

7 It will probably take several seasons before the plants knit together to form a living carpet so, although not essential, you may prefer to use a decorative mulch such as chipped bark to improve the overall appearance.

Making Borders

In general, try to match the size of your border to the amount of time and energy you can devote to it. At the same time, however, you should try to make its physical proportions match those of the house and the garden as a whole.

MOWING EDGE

1 Lay the paving slabs on the grass for positioning, and use a half-moon edger to cut a new edge.

2 Slice off the grass with a spade, and remove enough soil for a layer of about an inch of sand and gravel mix, mortar and the slabs. Consolidate the sub-base.

3 Use five blobs of mortar on which to bed the slab, and then tap the paving level using a mallet or the handle of a club hammer.

4 Make sure the slabs are flush with the lawn, and use a spirit level to check that the slabs are laid evenly. Mortar the joints for a neat finish, otherwise weeds will grow in them.

MAKING A BORDER IN A LAWN

A linear shape, rectangular or square, with straight edges is the traditional choice for a formal border. Such a border is usually edged with brick or paving to make an edge for the mower and reduce the maintenance in the garden. The plants in the border can flow over its edge onto the brick or paving and will not be damaged by, nor in the way of, the mower. A formal straight-edged border should be of substantial width, so that it makes an impact with the planting you choose. If the border is narrow, it will not have the depth for several changes of height, nor for the pools of color that make such borders so attractive to look at.

To begin with, you will have to lift the turf. Mark out the shape of the border using pegs and string lines if it is to be linear in shape. If the border is to be curved or circular, use a piece of hosing to mark it out, within a linear framework. This makes it easier to remove the turf. Then you can put the turf back at the edges of the circle.

Using a semi-circular bladed edging tool, cut out several rows of turf to make it easier to lift them. To lift away each turf, use a sharp-edged spade or a turfing spade to slide under the turf surface. As far as possible, avoid treading on the newly-opened soil surface, or you will compact it more than it already is.

When you have lifted sufficient turf, you will need to aerate the soil. Double dig it, fork it over and then add well-rotted manure or compost to it to give it a good texture and to give the plants a good start. Whatever type of soil predominates in your garden,

for the best results in terms of plant growth, it needs to be open and have a good texture so that the roots can get well down into it and become established. Double digging to a depth of 18-24in should do this. The soil should also be well drained. If necessary, you may need to dig in drainage channels, or add grit or sand to the soil when you double dig, to improve drainage.

After double digging, leave the soil to settle over the autumn, and in winter the action of frost and rain will make the soil more friable and crumbly. A traditional term for this is hazelling: the soil wrinkles and crumbles, looking like the rough brown skin of a hazel nut. The action of earthworms and other soil organisms also helps to improve the soil's condition.

As they grow, plants will need nutrients throughout a long growing period and this should be dug in as compost or manure when you prepare new ground. Or you can add it to the border in spring as a compost mulch. Mulching will also help to protect the soil surface, preventing it from drying out in periods of drought, and once the compost mulch is dragged down into the soil, it will offer nutrients in the soil to the plant.

An attractive edging of brick.

RENOVATING A PREVIOUSLY CULTIVATED BORDER

When renovating a previously cultivated border, you have to improve the soil condition. Dig out all perennial weeds such as bindweed, dandelion, common dock and nut grass. These are invasive weeds that will take some work to get rid of, since any part that breaks off can become a weed plant in its own right. The best time to remove such weeds is in the spring when their growth is fresh and the soil friable enough to dig over. You can also weaken them by laying black plastic across the site for a few weeks, so depriving them of light. Before you start on the border, lift the plastic and dig out the feeble strands on the weeds.

Perennial weeds with long tap roots, such as dock, should be levered out with a fork. It is easy to remove them when they are young in the spring and when the ground is moist just after a spring shower. To prevent a huge crop of them from year to year, remove the flowerheads and seeds of any that get away before you dig them out.

You will also need to remove stones and other debris. If there are any existing plants that you want to save, dig them out and heel them into a holding bay in another part of the garden until you are ready to add them to the new planting.

MAKING A GRAVEL BORDER

Gravel beds provide an attractive site and considerably reduce the maintenance in terms of weeds. A gravel bed also offers the perfect site for plants such as grasses, lavender, yucca and many alpines that prefer well-drained, dry conditions.

A gravel border is normally used for a small collection of plants and makes a change of pace between intensive flower and foliage planted borders. Gravel can also be used in place

GRAVEL BEDS

1 Mark out the bed with rope, a hose or by sprinkling sand where you think the outline should be. Check you are happy with its position and size. Then cut the outline of the bed using a half-moon edger. A spade will do, but this does not produce such a crisp edge.

2 Lift the grass within the bed with a spade, removing about 4in from the surface. The finished bed must be a couple of inches below the grass, otherwise the gravel will spill onto the lawn and damage the mower.

of lawn and paths, giving the impression of a dry river bed, with the border plants as islands of color. It is a perfect surface for plants to self-seed into, and it is easy to take any that are too

3 Spread a generous quantity of garden compost or rotted manure over the surface, and add a slow- or controlled-release fertilizer. Then fork this in to loosen and enrich the soil. If the ground is poorly drained and you want to grow dry soil plants, work in plenty of coarse grit too. This is an important stage as it is difficult to improve the soil once the gravel is in place.

abundant and replant them elsewhere. When you begin to plant the border, use a fork or a trowel to remove the layer of gravel, make slits in the membrane and dig a planting hole.

Above: *A graveled area. Gravel beds can be heavily planted with a combination of drought-resistant plants. The weed-suppressing gravel will mean they mainly look after themselves.*

4 Spread about 2in of gravel over the soil, making sure it is kept off the lawn and will not spill onto it.

Annual Border

Bright and cheery annual flowers provide the quickest and easiest color in a flower border, and they are also useful as seasonal fillers in a perennial border.

Annual is the term used to describe plants that are sown every year and that grow, flower and set seed all in the same year. There are many annuals to choose from to achieve a colorful, but seasonal, display in the garden. Some can be sown directly into their growing sites, while others, known as half-hardy annuals, need cosseting with warmth and protection before they are planted out into the warm soil in spring. If you want to, you can sow hardy annuals into trays in a greenhouse to plant out when the soil warms up again, but unless you have both the time and the resources, this is not necessary.

Instead, rake the already prepared soil in the border until there is a fine tilth. Then decide where you want different blocks of color, and of course, bear in mind the varying heights and spaces that should be allocated to different plants. Use a cane to mark out various shapes in the soil. These will then be the sites for sowing. Within each block, mark out parallel lines or drills along which you will sow the seed. Most annual seed should be sown to a depth of ¼–½in and in rows that are evenly spaced to 8-12in apart.

Sowing into neat rows in blocks means that in a few weeks' time, when the seed has germinated, it will be instantly recognizable and stand out from any annual weed seeds that will have germinated as well. It will be easy to hand weed at this stage and also to thin out seedlings from overcrowded rows. Leave space in the planting scheme to allow for the half-hardy annuals that you have sown in the greenhouse, and when the plants are large enough, plant them out into their growing site.

Watering is necessary while the plants become established, particularly in dry seasons, but beyond that, the only maintenance is to deadhead and tidy up the plants as they grow. The more you deadhead the plant, the more flowering is encouraged. During the summer it will give the plants an extra boost if you give them liquid feed when you water. At the end of the flowering season leave some of the flowers to develop seeds and in this way some of your work next year will have already be done for you, when the self-sown seedlings germinate in spring.

There is an extenisve range of

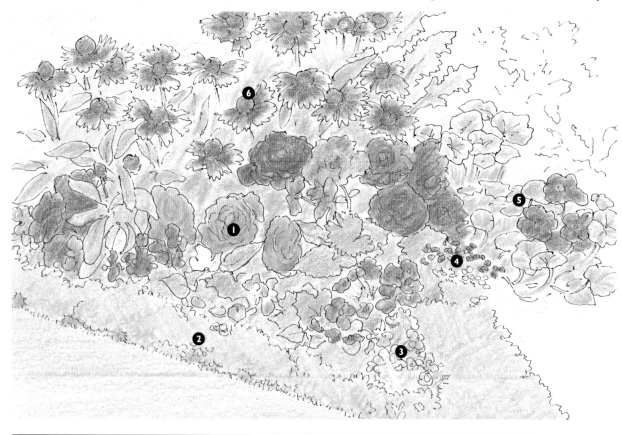

PLANT LIST

1 *Begonia* 'Non-Stop Mixed' hybrids
2 *Tanacetum* 'Santana Lemon'
3 *Begonia* 'Burgundy'
4 *Lobelia erinus compacta* 'Blue Wings'
5 Rowan (*Tropaeolum*) 'Alaska'
6 *Gaillardia* hybrids

plants and colors available, and the seed companies are continually extending their lists with new and improved seed strains. Some offer color-coordinated selections with a range of heights, so that you can easily achieve a harmonious effect just by sowing into different parts of the border.

Below: *In this vibrant border, hardy and half-hardy annuals are used in combination with the perennial blanket flower, Gaillardia hybrids. At the edge, the half-hardy annual,* Tanacetum *'Santana Lemon' is growing as a low frame. The half-hardy annual* Begonia *'Non-Stop Mixed' rises above the smaller-flowered, fibrous-rooted* half-hardy Begonia *'Burgundy'. Half-hardy* Lobelia erinus compacta *'Blue Wings' and hardy annual* Nasturtium (Tropaeolum) *'Alaska' tumble over the paving and the bright display is backed by a group of perennial blanket flowers,* Gaillardia *hybrids.*

Herbaceous Borders

Herbaceous plants need to be chosen with care. Some well-behaved, no-fuss but showy plants are suggested here but there are many more. If in doubt, always find out whether the plant needs staking, how fast it spreads and whether it is prone to pests and diseases. Border phlox and perennial asters are prone to mildew, for example.

PLANTING A BORDER

After the initial planting, your border will need little care to keep it looking good.

1 Always make sure the pots have been watered before planting, otherwise the root-ball may remain dry as water runs off it when watering after planting.

2 Space the plants out in their pots before you start to plant, as changes are easy at this stage. Try to visualize the plants at their final height and spread, and don't be tempted to plant them too close.

3 Knock the plant out of its pot only when you are ready to plant, so that the roots are not exposed unnecessarily to the drying air. Carefully tease out some of the roots.

4 Plant small plants with a trowel, large ones with a spade, and always work methodically from the back, or from one end of the border.

5 Return the soil and make sure the plant is at its original depth or just a little deeper. Firm it with your hands or a heel to expel large pockets of air in the soil.

6 Water thoroughly unless the weather is wet. Be prepared to water regularly in dry weather for at least the first few weeks after planting.

RELIABLE AND EASY PLANTS

It's worth including some of the following plants on your shopping list, but add others to suit the size of your border and to reflect your own taste.

Agapanthus (not for cold areas)
Alchemilla mollis (may self-sow so be prepared for seedlings)
Anemone × *hybrida*
Anthemis tinctoria
Astilbe
Bergenia (a non-woody evergreen)
Catananche caerulea
Dianthus (a non-woody evergreen)
Dicentra spectabilis
Echinops ritro
Erigeron
Hemerocallis
Kniphofia
Liatris spicata
Lilium
Liriope muscari
Lobelia cardinalis
Polemonium caeruleum
Schizostylis coccinea
Veronica spicata

GARDENER'S TIP

You can buy pot-grown herbaceous plants at any time of the year, but spring or autumn are the best times to plant.

Right: *Herbaceous borders will need less care if you plant large clumps of fewer kinds rather than lots of different ones that will need more frequent attention.*

Mixed Borders

Don't be too rigid about the plants that you use or mix in beds and borders. Herbaceous and non-woody evergreens can be useful ground cover around shrubs, while some shrubs, such as rue, can often be mistaken for herbaceous plants when used among them. Sometimes a mixed border containing both shrubs and herbaceous plants can bring out the best in both. If there are any gaps left because the plants are still small, don't hesitate to sow some bright annuals instead of leaving bare soil for weeds to colonize.

Above: *This very narrow bed shows how charmingly shrubs and herbaceous plants may be combined. However, if slugs are a problem in your garden, you may find the hostas an unwise choice.*

Astilbe chinenis 'Pumila'

Above: *Hostas have been planted at the front of this mixed border. The height differential means that you have the benefit of two borders in one, as the hostas in front do not mask the tall plants behind.*

Right: *Plants such as Astilbe and Potentilla add color to mixed borders and can largely be left to their own devices.*

Potentilla 'Tangerine'

Right: *This narrow border is only about 4 ft wide, but herbaceous perennials have been allowed to tumble over at the front to provide useful color contrasts with the yellow shrub behind. This is the evergreen* Choisya ternata *'Sundance' with* Aster novi-belgii *'Audrey' (left) and 'Jenny' (right) and a pink chrysanthemum in the center. In front is a pink-flowered rock rose that would have bloomed in late spring and early summer. This kind of combination of shrubs and herbaceous plants ensures season-long color.*

Spring Color

Freshness and vitality are the keynotes of spring borders. Bright yellow narcissi, white and green-tipped snowdrops, soft mauve crocuses and the rainbow colors of tulips are all popular choices.

Regularity and uniformity of planting are often associated with spring schemes. Tulips or narcissi rise high on their long stems above a mass of frothy bedding plants such as forget-me-not, *Myosotis.* It is as if we are imposing a strict management on the waywardness of what are essentially garden versions of wild spring flowers, wehich have been tamed through intensive breeding endeavors for our borders.

Here in the garden recreated at the home of the French Impressionist painter, Monet, in Giverny, France, that regularity and single-minded planting of just two or three different plants provides a sense of infinite space, as well as infinite resources of labor and finance.

The soft-colored gravel of the hard landscaping in the path defines the border edges clearly. The main plant choices offer a unity of color and continue the regularity established by the path. Their varying heights and flower colors, though, relieve the monotony of this uniform look and make for a natural rhythm. Edging the long lines of the beds, and making a soft line with the path is the low-growing, mound-forming favorite of spring, *Lobularia maritima* 'Royal Carpet'. Its curved outline spills out of the bed and softens the edge of the path, linking it with the planting.

Soft, billowy white and pale blue, tall bearded iris flowers float high above their angular, lance-like leaves in spring, imitating some exotic butterfly. Before the flowers appear, the fresh green and uniform shape of the foliage plays its own part in the border's overall look. Making a softer contrast are the more natural-looking flowers of the Siberian wallflower, *Erysimum hieraciifolium,* on the left of the path, and the scented wallflower, *Cheiranthus cheiri* on the right. Both are perennials, but in spring bedding schemes they are treated as annuals.

Above: *In contrast to the regularity of the spring border at Giverny, a more natural effect is achieved by the mass planting of spring-flowering bulbs and perennials. Here purple crocus and yellow aconites show their faces above the marbled leaves of* Arum italicum pictum, *while the rich mauve flowers of hellebores stand atop their leafless stems. In the background are green-tipped white bells of snowdrops.*

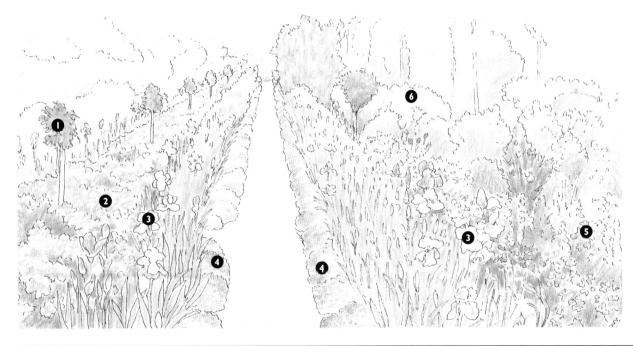

PLANT LIST
1 Standard roses
2 *Erysimum hieraciifolium*
3 Tall bearded iris in blue and white
4 *Lobularia maritima* 'Royal Carpet'
5 *Cheiranthus cheiri*
6 *Hesperis matronalis*

Adding to the perfume of the wallflowers is the white-flowered form of dame's violet, *Hesperis matronalis,* with its head of massed small flowers. Once their flowers are over, they may seed, but will probably be cut back to allow the leafy rosettes to establish well for the following year's flowering.

To give the border height, there are regularly-spaced and very trimly-shaped standard hybrid tea roses that will flower on their round pom-pom-shaped heads in summer. All these plants, with their different colors and very different shapes and heights, planted out so repetitively, present a seemingly infinite perspective. Later, when the spring flush of flowering is over in this long border, the lobularia flowers will be cut off, probably in a back-breaking shearing over with pruners, and once it has recovered, the foliage will continue to edge the path.

The iris stems and foliage will have to be cut back to a traditional fan shape. The iris root or rhizome which rests just on the soil surface, will be able to bake in the summer sun, unshaded by the foliage of other plants, building up its resources for future spring flowering. The scented wallflower in this border is treated as an annual spring bedding plant; it will later be replaced by a similar summer bedding plant.

Below: Lobularia maritima *'Royal Carpet' spills across the gravel path, tall bearded blue and white iris, and a fragrant mass of Siberian wallflowers, scented wallflowers and* Hesperis matronalis *provide the spring color within the border.*

Summer Color

Flowers that make pools of color and shafts of sunlight over a long period are the most popular choice for pleasing effects in a stately summer border. To achieve this there is a wide choice of herbaceous perennial and annual material.

Using plants that offer either vertical or horizontal color, you can vary the pace of the border's planting. Here the wide, flat heads of closely-packed flowers of *Achillea* 'Cloth of Gold' sway on long stalks above the felt-like, slightly aromatic leaves to make a burst of sunlight-yellow. The streak of yellow is repeated through the border, sometimes with similar plantings of achillea or with sunny-colored but differently shaped flowers, such as those of *Verbascum* 'Gainsborough'. The candelabra-like flower stems of the verbascum will provide a different shape, but a similar

block of color, and make a break between the busier or more varied colors and hues of its neighboring plants.

Lowering the height, and thus the focal level, is a swathe of salmon and rosy pink Peruvian lilies, *Alstroemeria ligtu* hybrids. Lily-like, and with their foliage playing hardly any part in the planting, they tumble forwards in the border, separating the yellows and blues. Just as you have taken in the change of height, it rises again, this time with the stately mauve-pink flowers of *Salvia turkestanica* and the deep blue of *Delphinium* 'Fenella'. Holding the line of the

blue flowers, but moving lower in height are clumps of borage and the starry blue of *Anchusa*. *Papaver* 'Mrs Perry', with shapely foliage, holds the front of the border at this point.

The continuity of color and rhythmic alteration of height hold your attention and demand you shift your gaze, but at a measured and relaxed pace.

A herbaceous border, such as this, can never be described as low maintenance, as there is always a plant that needs deadheading, tying back or staking. Achillea and delphinium in particular should be staked, especially in exposed sites. It is

best to put the stakes or supports in place at the planting time or in spring each year, before the plants have begun to grow away. Then, when they do need the support, they will have grown into it and you will hardly see that it is there.

At its best between June and September, a summer herbaceous border is packed with more than just the plants you can see at any one moment during the season. This allows for some to come to maturity, and then when their blooms are spent, their place is taken, center stage, by a plant that has been waiting in the wings.

PLANT LIST
1 *Achillea* 'Cloth of Gold'
2 *Verbascum* 'Gainsborough'
3 *Delphinium* 'Fenella'
4 *Salvia turkestanica*
5 *Papaver* 'Mrs Perry'
6 *Anchusa azurea*
7 *Alstroemeria ligtu* hybrids
8 *Penstemon* 'Sour Grapes'
9 *Salvia uliginosa*
10 *Gaura lindheimeri*

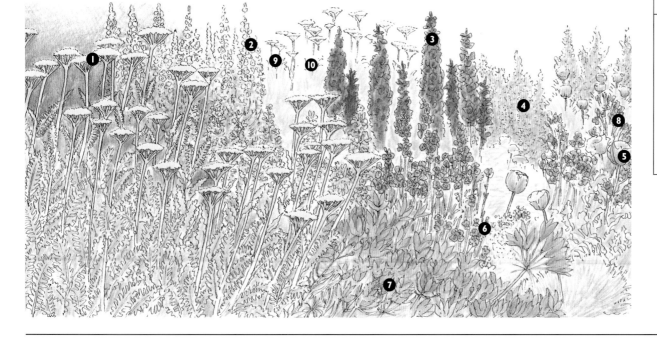

In this border the dancing blue flowers of *Salvia uliginosa* and the delicate, butterfly-like flowers of *Gaura lindheimeri*, wait their turn at the base of giant cardoons, planted through the border. To hold the blues and white of the flowers, and combine them with the gray of the cardoon foliage, *Penstemon* 'Sour Grapes', sparkles to life at the front of the border.

Below: Achillea *'Cloth of Gold' and* Verbascum *'Gainsborough' provide the sunlight, while lighter shades of mauve come from* Salvia turkestanica *and* Papaver *'Mrs Perry', making softer accents. Deep blue blocks of color are the offerings of* Delphinium *'Fenella' and* anchusa, *while a flame of salmon and rosy pinks lights the front of the border.*

Autumn Color

As late summer turns into mellow autumn, the colors in the border would seem to imitate the tawny colors of foliage, russet fruits and orange vegetables. Even the glow of autumn sunsets and misty early mornings finds an echo in the border.

One group of flowers in particular that fills the color gap between summer and winter comes from the daisy family – *Compositae.* Once known under such familiar names as chrysanthemum, they now belong to several genera whose names are as mellifluous and honeyed to roll off the tongue as the season itself. Dendranthema, argyranthemum and aster are among their number, with a range of bronze, yellow, mauve, white and ruddy flowers. The most important contribution this range of perennials makes to the autumn border is to maintain some color and interest for as long as possible beyond the full splendor of summer.

Mostly hardy, this group of flowers needs full sun or part-shade to grow well. Well-drained, enriched soil is best for them, but in dry summer seasons, they will need watering to prevent fungal outbreaks. With many species and cultivars growing to a considerable height and carrying flowers on every stem, they are bulky characters that need space for their tawny display to look its best. To keep them from flopping forward dramatically, they should be supported early on in their growing season.

Flowering over a long period, they need deadheading regularly, with their stems cut back to allow for new flowers on shorter spurs. Asters with their smaller, less densely packed flowerheads make a soft focus. In this planting, penstemons, the butterfly-attracting *Sedum spectabile* 'Brilliant' and the hybrid Japanese anemone, *Anemone* x *hybrida* 'Bressingham Glow', relieve the emphasis on asters and dendranthema.

Some forms of Michaelmas daisy, such as the modern *Aster novi-belgii* hybrids, are prone to mildew and insect attack and will need regular spraying with a fungicide. If the plants suffer badly, it is best to cut out affected stems, water well and continue the spraying regime.

Here they are planted together in a border that is more a demonstration garden, showing the range of colors available. In your own border, they can be combined and color-coordinated with other late-flowering autumn dazzlers including the white-flowered *Anemone japonica*

PLANT LIST
1 *Anemone* x *hybrida* 'Bressingham Glow'
2 *Dendranthema* 'Shining Light'
3 *Aster amellus* 'Jacqueline Genebrier'
4 *Penstemon* 'Thorn'
5 *Dendranthema* 'White Gloss'
6 *Aster lateriflorus* 'Datschii'
7 *Dendranthema* 'Doris'
8 *Dendranthema* 'Moonlight'
9 *Penstemon* 'Raven'
10 *Aster turbinellus*

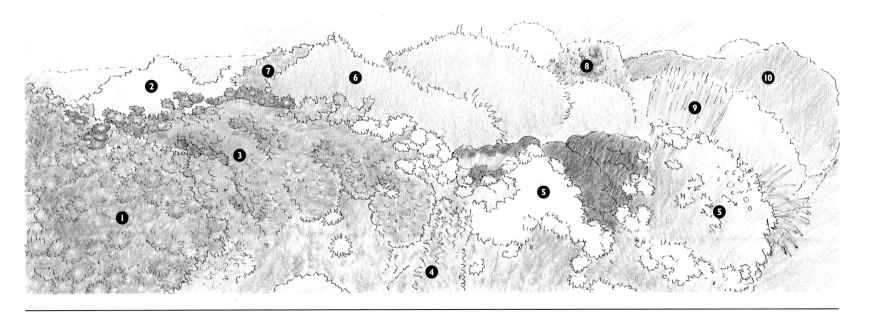

'Honorine Jobert' and the sunny yellow-flowered *Rudbeckia* 'Goldsturm'. The white-flowered *Achillea ptarmica* 'The Pearl' and *Campanula lactiflora*, with its branching flower stems in blue, white and sometimes pink blooms, are also good choices to prolong the flowering of the late summer border into autumn.

For the foreground, instead of sedum and penstemon, substitute hostas. *Hosta* 'Honeybells' and *H.* 'Green Fountain' provide particularly glowing foliage and useful flowers. For the background, the tall *Cephalaria gigantea* makes a bold display.

Left: *Their pink-mauve flowers blending so well together, the iceplant* Sedum spectabile *'Brilliant' and* Dendranthema *'Raquel' provide color at the front of the border over a long period during the autumn.*

Below: *At the Royal Horticultural Society Garden, Wisley, the late autumn border holds its own mellow display with Japanese anemone, penstemons, dendranthema and asters.*

Winter Color

Even in winter's depths there are shrubs and herbaceous perennials that will lighten the gloomiest of days and bring the border to life.

Now that summer and autumnal abundance are past, the border can no longer depend on flowers alone for its richness of color. Instead, bark, stems, foliage, berries, hips and seedheads, as well as the evergreen framework of hedges, are the factors that impress during this season.

Conifers, in a range of green, gold and even blue needle color, such as X *Cupresso-cyparis leylandii* 'Castlewellan', together with box, holly, privet and yew, provide the specimen plantings, as well as hedging and edging for the winter garden. But for flaming, glowing color, the winter stems of dogwood offer the brightest focus. Depending on form, there are stems in many shades of yellow-green and deep red. To ensure that they make the maximum impact, the plants should be stooled or cut back in spring, once their winter display is over. This encourages the growth of new stems throughout the season that will make the display so good the following winter, once their leaves have fallen.

Good stem color is also available from the ghost bramble, *Rubus cockburnianus* and *Rubus biflorus*, which make a frosty white tracery if planted in the border. The stems should be cut back in spring to encourage new growth, and to keep the plants in hand, although the ghost bramble is not as vigorous as the hedgerow bramble.

If there is space in the garden for trees, within or near the border, maples and birches offer a wonderful range of bark colors and textures.

In a winter border, the most important effect is that of light. In this border, the glow of ground-hugging ivy, *Hedera helix* 'Sagittifolia Variegata', lights the foreground. Moving upwards, the flower bracts of *Helleborus foetidus* take the brightness above their glossy, toothed leaves to the linear stems of the dogwoods, *Cornus alba* 'Sibirica' and *C. stolonifera* 'Flaviramea'.

For floral effects, winter-flowering heaths, such as *Erica* x *darleyensis* 'Darley Dale' or

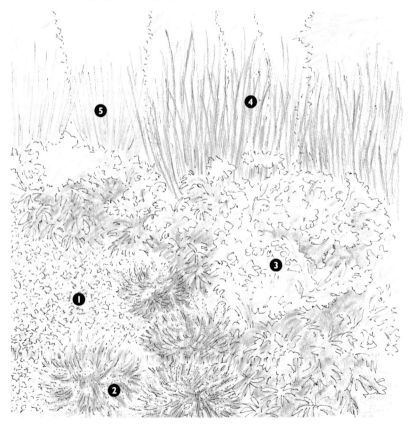

Left: *The flaming fiery colors of witch hazel,* Hamamelis x intermedia *'Jelena', are criss-crossed by the frosty stems of the ghost bramble,* Rubus biflorus. *In the foreground the little blue stem grass makes its autumn red foliage display, while* Erica x darleyensis *and winter-flowering aconites,* Eranthis hyemalis, *provide the floral effects.*

Opposite: *In the foreground, the variegated foliage of* Hedera helix *'Sagittifolia Variegata' makes a light carpet for* Erica carnea *'C.J. Backhouse'. Rising in a shimmering row above their dark green shining foliage, the flower bracts of* Helleborus foetidus *take the glowing color effect to the linear stems of two dogwoods. The light lemon-green of* Cornus stolonifera *'Flaviramea' and the red stems of* Cornus alba *'Sibirica' should be cut to ground level in spring to ensure a good growth of new stems for next winter's show.*

PLANT LIST

1 *Hedera helix* 'Sagittifolia Variegata'
2 *Erica carnea* 'C.J. Backhouse'
3 *Helleborus foetidus*
4 *Cornus alba* 'Sibirica'
5 *Cornus stolonifera* 'Flaviramea'

E. carnea 'C.J. Backhouse' with slightly differing mauve bell-shaped flowers, provide good ground cover and color at the base of trees and in the foreground of a border.

Small trees and shrubs that carry the floral effect through the season are useful in the border. The pink flowers of *Prunus* x *subhirtella* 'Autumnalis' float across this border, to make a high level floral focus. In the border there are many winter-flowering viburnums such as *Viburnum* x *bodnantense* with its fragrant flowers. For the most dazzling effects of all, witch hazels offer a sparkling firework display with their finely cut flowers in shades of orange, bronze and yellow.

Grasses, too, provide good color in winter. Some, such as the little blue stem grass, *Schizachyrium scoparium*, have foliage and stems that change color. The spring and summer blue-green of this grass's stems and foliage turns red in autumn and winter, and if planted fairly densely, will make a strong impact in an informal border.

Incidental effects are also part of the winter display. Seedheads, foliage, stems and evergreen hedging and edging are all transformed into a winter wonderland when the first frost occurs. Then the real bones and framework of the garden are highlighted by a delicate, but ephemeral tracery, that disappears as the winter sun warms the day.

Rose Border

Roses once used to be grown in separate borders devoted solely to their cultivation. In such a border, their summer glory could be admired, but after flowering, their thorny, bare stems and falling foliage in autumn looked unattractive.

Today in most domestic gardens the rose has come in from the cold and joined the party in the flower border with other plants. Old roses, in particular, need good herbaceous partners. Beautiful and fragrant they may be when in flower during high summer, but their season of beauty is short and soon they need the cluster of companions to disguise their own shortfalls.

However, while they are in flower there are so many herbaceous perennials, as well as annuals, that look attractive with them, that it is worthwhile choosing plants to complement and harmonize with the full fragrant blooms of the old roses. The range of plants that mix happily with roses is wide. Ground-covering, softly pastel-flowered geraniums such as

Above: *The soft full blooms of* Rosa *'Comte de Chambord' are enhanced by the edging of upright, blue spikes of* Lavandula *'Hidcote'*.

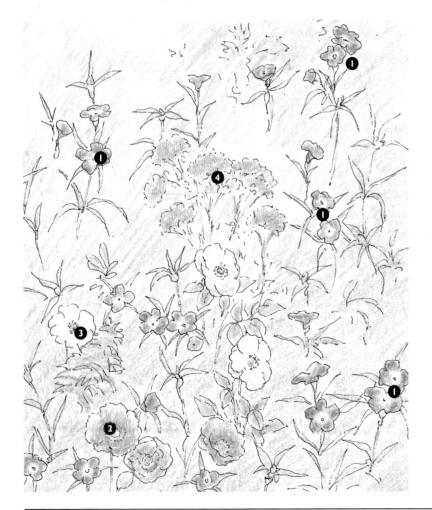

PLANT LIST

1 *Agrostemma githago*
2 *Papaver rhoeas* 'Mother of Pearl'
3 *Rosa* 'Iceberg'
4 *Thalictrum aquilegiifolium*

Geranium endressii, Geranium pratense 'Mrs Kendal Clarke' and *Geranium phaeum* in its white or purple form, and *Alchemilla mollis* and primulas are good companions in season.

Tall spires of white or mauve foxgloves are the romantic's choice for a rose border, but for lower cover around the roses, the red, button-like flower of *Knautia macedonica* on long thin stems is attractive. Lamium with its streaky silver-leaved and pink-hooded flowers is good at ground level, while phlox in white or shades of pink and penstemon in pink, mauve and burgundy make a pleasing contribution at mid-height.

In this border, a romantic, painterly look has been created using delicately colored annuals. The natural, simple flowers of corn cockle, *Agrostemma githago,* which grows to 3ft and carries its pastel flowers on will-o'-the-wisp stalks, rise above the white blooms of *Rosa* 'Iceberg'. Taking up the same pastel shades, but with a metallic finish, are the delicate papery blooms of the poppy, *Papaver rhoeas* 'Mother of Pearl'. Taller perennials such as *Thalictrum aquilegiifolium*, with its silvery foliage and frothy flowers, rise even higher above the cultivated former cornfield flowers and roses. Hollyhocks, dame's violet and silene are also planted in the border and there are low-

Right: *A painterly image is created by mixing corn cockle* Agrostemma githago *with the metallic poppies 'Mother of Pearl' and sowing them into the same border as delicately scented white* Rosa *'Iceberg'.*

growing miniature roses to enjoy at a lower level in the mixed herbaceous border. Unlike old roses, the miniatures will flower over a long period, and some, depending on the species and type, offer small, often bronze-edged foliage.

Although the under- and inter-planting of roses with many other plants may make rose maintenance slightly more difficult, it is worthwhile for the longer flowering and the harmonious combinations which can be achieved. Spring bulbs, including crocus and snowdrops, and spring bedding such as aubrieta and violas will also suit the base of roses.

Roses will thrive if they can be mulched around their roots in spring, so avoid planting them too closely. If you need to spray during the growing season, avoid doing so on hot or windy days as you may damage the surrounding plants. Regular deadheading, and for old roses, cutting out of spent canes and tying or shortening of whippy new growth, is necessary. Old roses also look attractive if their stems are arched and tied down to encourage more flower stems to break along the branch.

Foliage Border

Shape, color, texture, architectural stature and delicate accents are just some of the ornamental offerings that plants grown more for their foliage than their flowers make to the border's beauty.

Sometimes the foliage effects come from plants that do not flower, or whose flowers are considered secondary, such as those of the plantain lily or hosta. In most cases, plants are chosen for a combination of their attributes, but those with good foliage earn their place in the border with great ease.

Evergreen foliage in its various colors and variegations makes up the permanent framework in the planting scheme. But plants such as ferns or hostas, whose fronds and leaves die down each year, offer an extra dimension. As they unfurl, the curving fronds or, in the case of hosta, rolled leaves, provide a sort of foretaste of their future size and texture. Later, when it is fully open and mature, hosta foliage makes an architectural impact. Ferns, so useful in shady, damp areas, offer a more delicate tracery.

Hostas are used here to make a bold, shapely block of color and are available in a variety of leaf colors including golden, waxy-blue and variegated creamy white and green. They make a ruff-like edge to the border, shaping it and screening the feet of neighboring plants.

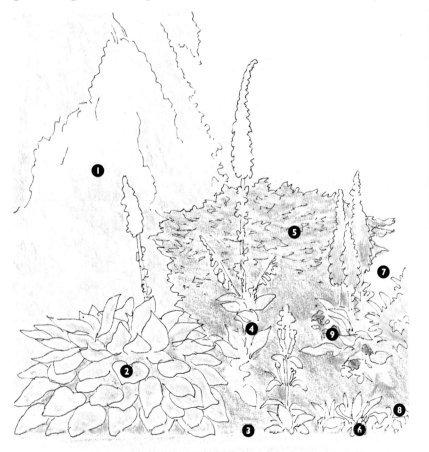

PLANT LIST
1 Betula pendula 'Youngii'
2 Hosta fortunei aureomarginata
3 Sedum maximum 'Atropurpureum'
4 Digitalis purpurea 'Alba'
5 Acer palmatum atropurpureum
6 Stachys byzantina
7 Iris foetida
8 Heuchera 'Pewter Moon'
9 Geranium 'Johnson's Blue'

Above: *Layer on layer of hosta foliage crowds the edge of the border, making a strong architectural impact through the growing season.*

Opposite: *Although there are flowering plants in this section of the border, the main impact comes from the color and shapes of the plant foliage.*

Good foliage effects can be had from plants with colored leaves. Purple foliage from the smoke bush, *Cotinus coggygria,* purple sage, dwarf berberis clipped into formal shapes and the deep purples of acers all offer excitement and good foliage accents to the border. Likewise, golden foliage provides color and texture. Some golden-leaved plants such as golden marjoram need to be grown in shade to protect their foliage from sun scorch.

Midway between green and gold, the lemony-green, furry leaves of *Alchemilla mollis* have an extra delight. At each leaf's center there is a small depression, and this holds drops of dew, like a little cup. Once this dew was thought to be the purest for washing the face.

In autumn, the real show-stoppers in the border come out in force. Acers, grasses and small trees and shrubs take on their seasonal color before losing their leaves. In this border, the purple-leaved *Acer palmatum atropurpureum* becomes fiery red and if it is planted so that it is backlit with the low-setting sun, it becomes almost incandescent. Some forms of *Acer palmatum* turn gold, others orange or red. Hostas lose the chlorophyll in their leaves and become an attractive yellow.

In this border, the foliage of the hostas cools down the purple of the acer and makes a good contrast for the small leaves of the weeping birch whose shape and bark are such strong features in the border. In autumn, the yellow of the hosta and red of the acer fight it out in the fading sunlight, glowing when all the herbaceous perennials have been cut back.

Island Border

Offering a greater challenge to the border gardener, curved island beds that can be viewed from all around the site have become a popular alternative to a traditional, linear formal border.

Unlike the formal border, which is viewed from the front with plants graded from low to tall and planted from front to back, the island border has to have an all-around focus and design.

Although there may be repeats of color blocks and groupings in an island bed, it is unlikely that it will have as strictly a repeated planting scheme as a more traditional formal border.

Instead, depending on the size and shape of the island, there will be two or three groups of taller plants, or even one or two specimen trees or shrubs, set roughly in the central area of the

Opposite: The curved shape and irregular height gradation make an island border less formal. It is challenging to plant in the round – every angle has to hold something of interest for the gardener and the garden visitor.

bed. The other plants will be arranged in sections, following an informal height gradation.

In these borders the height and central interest is achieved by planting ornamental shrubs or trees, stooled to produce multi-stems. For example, *Sambucus nigra* 'Pulvurulenta', a form of elder with its green leaves striped and mottled white, is cut back hard in spring, to encourage growth of stems bearing its attractive foliage. In the border beyond, *Populus serotina* 'Aurea', the golden Italian poplar, is growing as a small bushy tree, but it could be stooled or pollarded to produce stems with its handsome yellow foliage. This poplar turns a yellow-green through the season, until in autumn it produces golden-yellow hues. Both are unusual choices for an island border and they make a distinctive show in the season. In winter, until cut back in spring, their stems make a

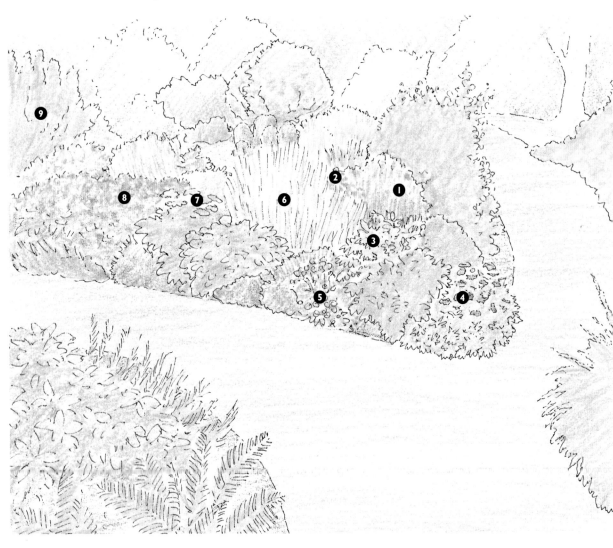

PLANT LIST
1 *Salvia guaranitica*
2 *Lobelia cardinalis*
3 *Polygonatum hybridum*
4 *Osteospermum jucundum*
5 *Origanum laevigatum* 'Herrenhausen'
6 *Iris pseudacorus* 'Variegata'
7 *Ligularia dentata* 'Desdemona'
8 *Persicaria amplexicaulis* 'Atrosanguinea'
9 *Populus serotina* 'Aurea'

framework for frost patterns if the season is severe.

The floral color in the island bed comes from plants including the technically half-hardy *Salvia guaranitica*. Here it has proved hardy, but cuttings are taken each year as an insurance policy, and other parts of the garden are filled with this deep blue sage that blooms from late summer till November. Other half-hardy plants include the mauve *Osteospermum jucundum*.

Although some of the half-hardy plants in the bed have survived numerous winters, it is always worth taking cuttings to ensure that you have new plants in case they do not survive. Apart from stooling the golden poplar and planting in the half-hardies in late spring to early summer, the border needs deadheading, mulching in spring, and dividing in autumn to stay in good heart.

Hardy perennials in the island bed include the deep red-flowered and purple foliage *Lobelia cardinalis,* the purple-flowered ornamental marjoram, *Origanum laevigatum* 'Herrenhausen', *Ligularia dentata* 'Desdemona' and *Iris pseudacorus* 'Variegata'.

Circular Border

Sometimes the form of a border is as breathtaking as the plant combinations that fill it, and here the concept of a border in the round is taken beyond the limits of simply an island of plants.

PLANT LIST

1 *Clematis* 'Victoria'
2 *Miscanthus sinensis* 'Cascade'
3 *Veronica virginica*
4 *Phlox paniculata* 'Elizabeth Arden'
5 *Monarda* 'Balance'
6 *Tradescantia* 'Zwanenburg Blue'
7 *Delphinium* 'Piccolo'
8 *Thalictrum aquelegifolium*
9 *Monarda* 'Scorpion'
10 *Galega hartlandii* 'Lady Wilson'

Above: *One of the many sitting places in the garden has a view over the inner pool area.*

Above: *The inner triangular paths seem to be as curved as the outer path, but it is actually an illusion created by the circular retaining wall and the soft overspilling of the plants.*

The photograph (right) shows a section of a circular border with a concentric circular path going nearly all the way around it. A concentric border, 6ft deep, planted with colors that correspond to those of the inner circle, lies inside the path. The circles are further emphasized by the 36-pole pergola circle and the circular retaining wall and pond terrace at the center of the garden. The inner circular border, large in its scope but treated in essence like a long border that has been curved back on itself, is crossed by two sets of paths that make their own contrasting double triangular shape on the design.

On paper, the intellectual geometry of the border is easy to grasp and once it is filled with the plants, combined so well and on so many different levels, the extraordinary harmony and symmetry of the garden reveals an overlay of color, texture and fragrance. There are nine distinct color schemes in the inner circle. The starting point for the different color schemes are the colors of the six *Buddleia davidii* planted at intervals on the inside of the pergola. They include 'Empire Blue', 'Pink Beauty', 'White Cloud', 'Black Knight', 'Summer Beauty' and 'Purple Prince'.

Each section is color-coordinated with its neighboring section, so that although the different sections are distinct,

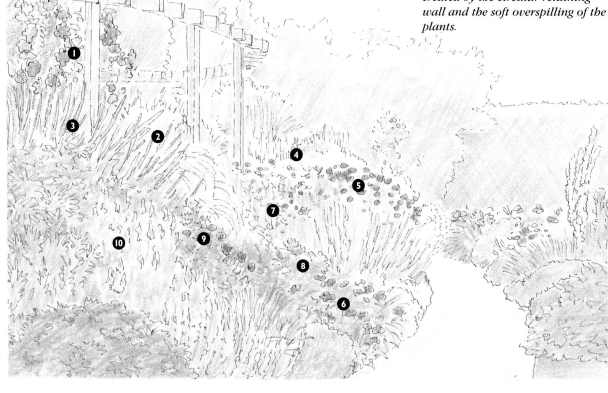

they also merge with each other. Plants in the outer sections are tall or medium-tall in height, so that as you curve along the circular path, outside the border, you can only see in to a certain level. Beyond the screen of plants is the rest of the border, but from the outside you can only guess at it, so retaining an element of surprise and interest in what is to come.

When you have crisscrossed the circular garden on the triangular paths, and walked the whole of the curved exterior path, there are numerous seats to find, as well as the sunken terrace at the garden's heart.

In this lower terrace there are some plants, mostly sun-loving Mediterranean varieties, grouped together in pots. The space in this area, the ability to look back at the border from an area without plants and the enjoyment of the small pool, make a tranquil garden. As you walk along the curved path, there is only one section of the border in view at any time, and you are always being invited to move on to view more, just around the corner.

Above: *As you walk along the curved outer path, only two borders are visible: the exterior one and the low- to medium-height plants of the outer section of the circular border. The taller plants at the foot of the pergola, and those that clothe the pergola itself, act as a screen to protect the privacy of the inner part of the garden.*

Romantic Border

Soft colors, fragrance, walls draped with swags of abundant blooms and beds filled with all the choicest of summer-flowering roses, peonies and iris are just some of the pointers to an informal and romantic style.

Although formal in their individual shapes, the character of the borders in this small walled garden is one of soft, romantic informality. Nearly all the wall space surrounding the borders is covered with climbers or wall plants such as *Ceanothus* 'Cascade', the white-flowered potato climber *Solanum jasminoides* and numerous clematis, all softening the texture of the hard landscaping. The impression is of a wall hung with generously draped, floral-printed textiles. The plants in each of the beds echo the colors of the "wall hangings" and in a

way become more like soft furnishings than plants.

In spring, the box-edged beds are filled with single color tulips, pink double early flowering *Tulipa* 'Angelique' and *Tulipa* 'White Triumphator', as well as Barnhaven primulas and numerous irises including 'Jane Phillips', 'Black Hills' and 'Braithwaite'. In early summer, peonies, including 'Duchesse de Nemours', 'Mrs Perry' and 'Cedric Morris', and roses come to the fore. Lavender takes the floral fragrance forward until the lilies, including 'Journey's End' and 'Sans Souci', open their

PLANT LIST

1 *Clematis* 'Henryii'
2 *Ceanothus* 'Cascade'
3 *Abelia grandiflora*
4 *Senecio* 'White Diamond'
5 *Hebe* 'Red Edge'
6 *Rosa* 'Gertrude Jekyll'
7 *Lavendula* 'Hidcote'
8 *Rosa* 'Queen of Denmark'
9 *Papaver orientale* 'Mrs Perry'
10 *Papaver* 'Cedric Morris'
11 *Rosa* 'Magenta'
12 *Buddleia* 'Nanho Blue'
13 *Artemisia ludoviciana*
14 *Juniperus scopulorum* 'Skyrocket'
15 *Rosa* 'Reine Victoire'
16 *Rosa* 'Heritage'
17 *Sisyrinchium striatum*
18 *Rosa* 'Constance Spry'
19 *Rosa* 'Mme Albert Carrière'

sumptuous blooms to overwhelm with their beauty and fragrance.

The softness of the blooms and shapes of the old roses within the beds is contrasted with the tall upright flower spikes of foxgloves in white and purple, and the creamy yellow of *Sisyrinchium striatum*. The contrasting nature of the soft foliage of roses and lavender, and the spiky foliage of sisyrinchium, as well as the iris, keep the style from becoming too sentimental. Similarly, anchoring the generous nature of the blooms in each of the beds, are plants with silver foliage. These plants are highly textured and they add to the already heady romance of the style, with their metallic coloring offering a glint of something rather more steely.

In keeping with the feel of the plants, the lion fountain and the white-painted wrought-iron bench offer the garden visitor a view into a less hurried and more indulgent world. On the surface, such a style looks easy to maintain, but behind the relaxed exterior there is a routine of regular maintenance.

In autumn, once plants die down they are cut back and tidied and manure is dug in around the plants, especially the roses. Old roses are cut back if their new growth is spindly, and lavenders are trimmed back, as are the box hedges. Clematis, depending on their flowering time, are cut back in autumn and spring and all climbing plants are tied in as they grow during the spring and summer.

Opposite: *The weathered statue of Flora is well-placed among sumptuous blooms of clematis, roses and geraniums.*

Below: *Evoking the essence of romance, of long summer nights and days. Fragrant roses, wall plants and pastel-colored perennials combine well to make a very particular garden style.*

Meditation Border

Depending on the mixture of plants and style, borders have varying effects on our senses. Some combinations of plants excite and stimulate, while others offer peace and tranquility – such as this border, created to be a place of meditation.

To create the right ambience for quiet repose only a few plants are necessary. Their large-scale planting does not allow for the visual or mental stimulation in the same way that a vibrant and floriferous border does and it allows the mind to be free, as is the eye, to roam back and forth along the edges of the paths, and there is plenty of space for thoughts and stillness.

This tranquil garden room is framed by high evergreen hedges of yew, *Taxus baccata,* on two sides and the conifer, *Thuja plicata* on one side (the fourth side is a wall of Kentish ragstone bricks or old Kent reds). The aim is to play down the senses and the energy that borders normally offer. Entering the garden is like coming upon a quiet, cloistered green room, set apart from the rest of the world. Even the seat, which is stonework from an old churchyard, contributes to the feeling of other worldliness.

The linear shapes of the paths and beds also contribute to the peaceful nature of the border. The tranquil planting is achieved by using *Alchemilla mollis* to line the border and to spill out onto the paths. Inside the lady's mantle edging are masses of Irish ivy, *Hedera helix* 'Hibernica'. The glossy leaves of the ivy contrast well with the soft and furry texture of the alchemilla leaves. The ivy is planted at a density of 30 plants per side and they took nearly three years to cover the ground allotted to them. Once or twice a year, they attempt to over-reach the space, and that is the time when they are cut back with a sharp spade.

The alchemilla was planted at a similar density and it is prevented from flopping over the path by a support of 15-in canes and garden twine. The flowers are cut off, which is a back-breaking exercise, in mid-July and new mounds of green leaves form. Although the alchemilla flowers offer a lime-yellow color, it is the calm green ivy foliage that predominates in this garden.

In the two box-edged rectangles at the end of the meditation garden, *Viola cornuta* is used as a ground cover and, when they are better established, the two variegated box plants in the center are to be trained as topiary columns.

In the late evening when the low-angled sun is setting, its rays light up the axis of the paths right up to the stone seat, giving the impression that it is more altar than seat. In the early morning too, the meditation garden has its special effects as the dew, held in the cupped foliage of *Alchemilla mollis,* dances with light.

PLANT LIST

1 *Alchemilla mollis*
2 *Hedera helix* 'Hibernica'
3 *Buxus sempervirens*
4 *Viola cornuta*

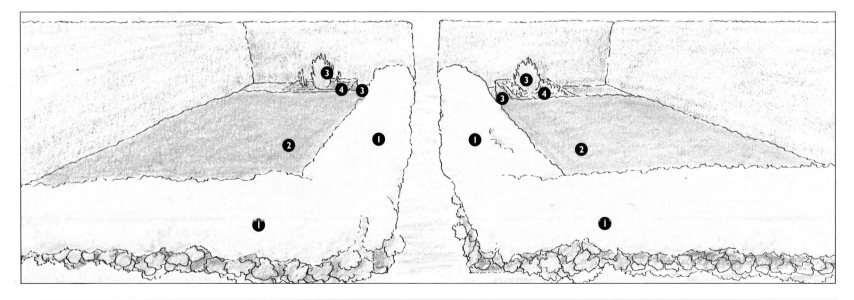

Right: *A simple plan of light and dark green plants, massed together, provided the inspiration for the meditation garden below.*

Below: *With no vibrant colors nor any dramatic changes in tempo or focus, the massed alchemilla and ivy plants allow for a calming of the senses and provide the precious time for quiet reflection.*

Container Gardening

Gardening in containers is the quickest, simplest and most economical way to transform your garden, especially when space is at a premium. A wide range of good-quality plants is available to every gardener all the year round, so that no corner need ever be overlooked or dull. There is no rule restricting you to plastic and earthenware pots, and this versatility, coupled with mobility, makes containers an inspirational resource for expert and novice alike.

Left: *Grouping containers together with imagination and flair can transform the plainest of spots.*

Above: *Less obvious containers such as this copper boiler make superb and unusual displays.*

Focus on Containers

If a plant is spectacular or a container interesting or eye-catching, it may be best to display it in isolation rather than in a group of plants or pots. Use it as a focal point to take the eye to a particular part of the garden. Or use them formally to flank a front door or guard a flight of steps.

Do not cover a spectacular container with trailing plants. Use upright plants that make the most of the container itself.

Garden objects from watering-cans to wheelbarrows make interesting containers. In a modern garden you can use modern objects, but in a country garden or one created in a rural or old-fashioned style, an old container may be more appropriate.

This old wooden wheelbarrow has long since been replaced by a lighter modern version, but with a coat of bright paint and a few drainage holes made in the bottom it will see many more years of decorative service.

Everyday objects such as old paint cans (though nowadays they are usually plastic) can be pressed into use with a little imagination. They will give your patio or garden that individual touch that bought containers simply cannot achieve. These two old paint containers have been painted white first, then had colored "drips" added to match the color of the gerberas.

Always make drainage holes in the base of containers that do not already have them before you plant them up.

There are some places where flowers will fail to thrive, but if the container is striking enough, you will not need them. The shrub border in this photograph was uninspiring before the addition of this large empty jar, which has transformed the area into one of great interest.

Above: *If both plant and container are big and bold, they do not have to be colorful or spectacular. This* Fatsia japonica *brings instant appeal to a shady part of the garden that would otherwise lack any points of interest.*

Left: *If the container is striking enough, the flowers can be almost coincidental. In fact, a very bold floral display may actually detract from a spectacular or unusual container.*

The container illustrated is eye-catching in both shape and color, and in its own way challenges the flowers to compete. This kind of container commands attention and takes the eye to that part of the garden. Avoid too many containers like this in close proximity, however, as they will vie for attention and the impact will be lessened.

Grouping Containers

Groups of containers are almost always more pleasing than single pots dotted around in isolation, especially if they are ordinary pots or service containers. You can hide quite ordinary containers behind smaller but more attractive ones by using a stepped effect, with the taller plants in bigger pots behind.

Sometimes choosing a group of containers with contrasting shapes and sizes can work, especially if they are used to add height and perhaps to fill in a visually bare area.

PLANTING A TUB OR URN

1 Even when containers are to be grouped, it is wise to include some mixed plantings instead of a separate pot for each plant. For these, choose a large pot or other container, and make sure there is a drainage layer of broken clay pots or something like coarsely chipped bark at the bottom.

2 Fill with a good quality potting soil. For seasonal plants a peat-based or peat-substitute compost will be satisfactory provided you feed frequently, but for shrubby plants or perennials, a loam-based potting soil is preferable. It will still require feeding, but the plants will be less prone to starvation.

Start with a tall plant in the center, always firming it in and making sure the top of the root-ball is covered with a good layer of potting soil.

3 Fill in with more plants around the edge to give the container a well-clothed look, but avoid trailers that will completely obscure an attractive pot like this, which deserves to be seen.

4 If the pot or container is attractive in its own right, make the most of it. Use mainly upright plants and position the container so that it is in a dominant position within the group.

However you arrange your containers, they should have a sense of harmony. Even if the plants are very different – and this group includes shrubs, succulents, bedding plants and border perennials – the use of decorative terracotta containers holds the collection together and gives the group unity.

Pots are usually grouped on a patio or paved area, and can transform an otherwise dull corner. The individual plants in this group of containers are unspectacular, but when displayed as a feature collectively they are just as attractive as a flowerbed. For groups in such a prominent position, however, it is necessary to rotate containers periodically so that there is always something interesting or seasonal to be seen. Unless you move a plant that has passed its best, it will mar the rest of the group.

Miniature Spring Garden

Terracotta pots filled with crocuses, irises and primroses, nestling in a bed of moss, make a delightful scaled-down spring garden which would fit on the smallest balcony or even a windowsill. Choose containers of contrasting shapes for best effect.

MATERIALS AND TOOLS
Terracotta seed tray
2 terracotta pots, 12 cm (5 in) high
Crocks
Standard soil mix
Sheet moss
Trowel

PLANTS
3 primroses
Pot of Reticulata irises in bud
Pot of crocuses in bud

crocus

Reticulata iris

sheet moss

primrose

GARDENER'S TIP

Once the irises and crocuses are past their best, hide them behind other pots to die down and dry out before starting them into growth again in the autumn.

Plant in early spring.

1 Cover the drainage holes of the seed tray and the two pots with crocks.

2 Half-fill the seed tray with soil mix. Before planting the primroses, loosen the roots by gently squeezing the root ball and teasing the roots loose. The plants will establish themselves far better in the surrounding soil mix if you do this.

4 Arrange the sheet moss around the plants so that all the soil mix is hidden.

5 Remove the irises from their plastic pot and slip them into the terracotta pot. Bed them in with a little extra soil mix if necessary and then arrange moss around the base of the stems.

3 Arrange the primroses in the seed tray and, once you are happy with their positioning, fill in with soil mix around the plants, pressing down around the plants to ensure they are firmly planted.

6 Repeat this process with the crocuses and then water all the pots.

GARDENER'S TIP

After the primrose plants have finished flowering they will send out glossy green leaves all summer long if they are kept in a cool shady spot and are watered regularly. Next year, after flowering they can be divided up to provide you with many more plants.

Spring Display in a Copper Boiler

A battered old wash boiler makes an attractive and characterful container for a display of white tulips underplanted with purple violets and evergreen periwinkles.

MATERIALS AND TOOLS
Copper boiler, 60 cm (24 in) diameter
Plastic pot, 20 cm (8 in) diameter
Standard soil mix
Trowel

PLANTS
20 white tulip bulbs or tulips in bud
5 purple violets
2 periwinkles (*Vinca minor* was used here)

tulip

periwinkle

violet

1 Place an upturned 20 cm (8 in) pot in the base of the boiler before filling it with soil mix. This will save on the amount of soil mix used and will not have any effect on the growth of the plants as they will still have plenty of room to grow.

4 Plant one violet in the center and four around the edges. Scoop out the soil by hand to avoid damaging the growing tips of the tulips beneath the soil.

2 If you are planting tulip bulbs, half-fill the container with soil mix, arrange the bulbs evenly over the surface and then cover them with a good 15 cm (6 in) of soil mix. This should be done in late autumn.

3 Do the underplanting in the early spring. The soil mix will have settled in the container and should be topped up to within 8 cm (3 in) of the rim. Remove the violets from their pots. Gently squeeze the rootballs and loosen the roots to aid the plants' growth.

5 Plant a periwinkle either side of the central violet, again loosening the rootballs.

GARDENER'S TIP

Lift the tulips when they have finished flowering and hang them up to dry in a cool airy place. They can be replanted later in the winter to flower again next year. Provided you pick off the dead flowers the violets will flower all summer. For a summer display, lift the central violet and plant a standard white marguerite in the center of the container.

Plant bulbs in autumn or plants in bud in spring. Plant the violets and periwinkle in spring.

6 Alternatively, if you are planting tulips in bud, the whole scheme should be planted at the same time. Work from one side of the pot to the other, interplanting the tulips with the violets and periwinkles. Press down firmly around the tulips or they will work themselves loose in windy weather. Position in sun or partial shade.

Auricula Theatre

In the late 18th and early 19th century "Primrose Feasts" were held, where prize auricula primroses were displayed in specially built theatres. This simple interpretation of an old tradition will create an interesting focal point in your garden.

MATERIALS AND TOOLS
Pine corner shelf unit
Steel wool or sandpaper
Paintbrush
Matt black exterior paint
Wall plugs and screws
Crocks
2 terracotta pots, 10 cm (4 in) high (preferably old)
Loam-based soil mix with ⅓ added grit

PLANTS
2 auricula primroses

auricula primrose

GARDENER'S TIP

An ordinary shelf unit will display the plants as effectively as a corner shelf. Use the theatre to display other dramatic plants when the auriculas are out of season: bright red geraniums, pot marigolds and nasturtiums in high summer, zinnias in late summer, and pansies during the autumn and winter.

Plant in spring.

1 Rub down the shelves with steel wool or sandpaper – this is particularly important if the wood has been treated with wax in the past.

2 Apply at least two coats of the paint to the shelves inside and out. Remember this is going to be outdoors and will need to be well sealed to protect it against the weather. Allow the paint to dry and then fasten it to the wall of your choice using wall plugs and screws.

3 Place a crock in the bottom of each terracotta pot. Gently remove each auricula from its plastic pot, supporting the plant as shown in the picture as the soil mix is likely to be quite crumbly.

4 Repot in the terracotta pots using some of the gritty soil mix to set it in firmly. Water immediately and frequently when they are on display. Auriculas do best in sun or partial shade.

Terracotta Planter of Spring Bulbs

This container of bright yellow tulips and daffodils will brighten the dullest spring day. The variegated ivies conceal the soil and pleasantly soften the edge of the planter.

MATERIALS AND TOOLS
Terracotta planter, 60 cm (24 in) long
Crocks or similar drainage material
Standard soil mix
Trowel

PLANTS
10 tulips
6 pots of miniature daffodils
6 variegated ivies

tulip

miniature daffodil

ivy

GARDENER'S TIP

Plant in early spring.

1 Fill the bottom of the planter with drainage material. Be especially careful to cover the drainage holes so that they do not become clogged with soil mix.

2 Remove the tulips from their pots and carefully separate the bulbs. Plant them in a staggered double row down the length of the planter.

3 Interplant the container with the miniature daffodils.

4 Finally plant the ivies around the edge of the planter. Remember that if you are using a planter like this as a window box, the back of the arrangement should look just as good as the front.

Seaside Garden

Even if you live miles from the sea you can create your own seaside garden in a sunny corner with some seashells, succulents and driftwood.

MATERIALS AND TOOLS
4 terracotta pots of various sizes
Seashells
Self-hardening clay
Loam-based soil mix with
    ⅓ added grit
Gravel
Driftwood
Trowel

PLANTS
Gazania
3 *Mesembryanthemum*
2 *Crassula*
Upright *Lampranthus*
2 trailing *Lampranthus*

Gazania

Lampranthus

1 Fill the back of the shells with clay, leaving some unfilled to cover the soil.

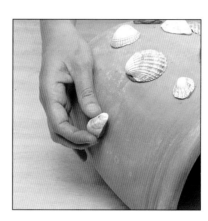

2 Press the shells onto the terracotta pots and leave the clay to harden overnight.

3 Plant the *Gazania* in one of the larger pots.

4 Plant the *Mesembryanthemum* as a group in one pot.

GARDENER'S TIP

Seaside plants are used to growing in difficult surroundings. Be careful not to kill them with too much kindness, and be especially careful not to overwater.

Plant in late spring or early summer.

5 Plant the *Crassula* together in a fairly small pot. These plants grow naturally in poor soils and do not mind a bit of overcrowding.

6 The upright and trailing *Lampranthus* have similar color foliage and flowers, but are quite different shapes so they make an interesting contrast when planted together. Cover the soil of each pot with a layer of gravel and then add seashells and pieces of driftwood. Group together in a sunny position.

Mediterranean Garden

The brilliant colors of the Mediterranean are re-created with these painted pots. The plants thrive in the climate of the Mediterranean, but will also perform well in less predictable weather.

MATERIALS AND TOOLS
4 terracotta pots of various sizes
Paintbrush
Selection of brightly colored emulsion
   paints
Masking tape
Crocks
Loam-based soil mix with
   ⅓ added grit
Gravel

PLANTS
Prostrate rosemary
Aloe
Golden thyme
Large red geranium

geranium

aloe

prostrate rosemary

golden thyme

1 Paint the pots with solid colors or with patterns. The paints used here are thicker than ordinary emulsion, so you may need two coats to get the same effect. The terracotta absorbs the moisture from the paint, so they will dry very quickly.

2 Paint the rim of one pot with a contrasting color.

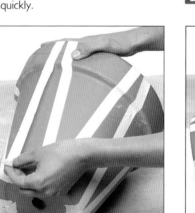

3 Create a pattern using tape to mask out specific areas.

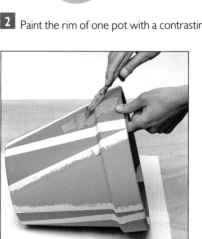

4 Paint every other area to create a zig-zag effect.

5 Place crocks in the bottom of the pots and then position the plants, firming them in place with extra soil mix. The roots of this rosemary are compacted and will benefit from being teased loose before planting.

GARDENER'S TIP

For commercial reasons the plants you buy will probably have been grown in a peat soil mix, although they prefer a loam-based soil mix. Gently loosen the peat around their roots and mix it with the loam-based soil mix before potting them up in the new mixture.

Plant in late spring or early summer.

6 The aloe does not need a large pot. Plant it in a pot just slightly larger than the one you bought it in.

7 Plant the thyme and geranium in separate pots. Finish the plants with a top-dressing of gravel, water well and place in a sheltered sunny corner.

Summer Flower Basket

The secret of a successful wall or hanging basket is to be generous with the plants. The result will then be a marvelous display of color which will last all summer long.

MATERIALS AND TOOLS
Wall basket, 30 cm (12 in) diameter
Terracotta or plastic pot (optional)
Sphagnum moss
Hanging basket soil mix
Slow-release plant food granules

PLANTS
6 lilac lobelia
3 pink petunias
2 *Convolvulus mauritanicus*
2 blue petunias
Lilac lantana
Trailing geranium

lobelia

lantana

petunia

Convolvulus mauritanicus

1 Rest your basket on a pot. This will hold it upright and allow you to work more easily.

2 Line the base of the basket and one-third of the way up the sides with a thick layer of moss.

3 Fill the moss-lined area with soil mix and plant four of the lobelia through the sides of the basket, so that their rootballs rest on the soil mix.

4 Add another layer of moss and soil mix, firming the remaining lobelias in as you work.

5 Just below the rim of the basket plant a pink petunia centrally with the *Convolvulus* at either side. Again introduce the plants through the sides of the basket.

GARDENER'S TIP

If you are going away for a week or two, move your baskets and container plants into a cool shady corner of the garden and water copiously before you leave. In cool weather they should stay in good condition until your return, and in hot weather your neighbours will only need to check them twice a week instead of daily.

Plant in late spring or early summer.

6 Add a further layer of moss and compost above these plants and plant the remaining petunias, the lantana and the geranium in the top of the basket, firming down well as you plant them. Scatter a tablespoon of plant food granules over the surface of the compost. This will feed the plants throughout the growing season. Water well before hanging the basket in a sunny position and then water daily in the morning or evening.

Wild Strawberry Basket

Wild strawberries can be grown in a basket and enjoyed anywhere, whether in the countryside or a small city garden.

MATERIALS
Wire basket, 30 cm (12 in) square
Sphagnum moss
Equal mix loam-based soil mix and
    container soil mix
Slow-release plant food granules
Trowel

PLANTS
4 Alpine strawberry plants

Alpine strawberry plant

GARDENER'S TIP

Propagate strawberry runners by pinning the plantlets into small pots of soil mix. A loop of wire or a hairpin either side of the plantlet will hold it firmly in place until it has rooted. Then simply cut the runner and you have a new, free strawberry plant.

Plant in spring to fruit in summer.

1 Line the basket with a generous layer of sphagnum moss.

2 Fill the lined area with soil mix. Scoop out a hollow for each strawberry plant, and press the soil mix firmly around the rootball as you plant.

3 Some of the plants may already be sending out runners. Make sure these hang over the edge of the basket so that as they grow they can be used to grow extra plants (see Gardener's Tip).

4 Scatter a tablespoon of plant food granules on the surface of the soil mix.

5 Tuck more moss around the edges of the basket and under the leaves of the plants. This will conserve moisture and stop the fruit touching the soil. Water and place in full or partial sun.

Galvanized Bath Garden

An old tin bath makes an ideal planter; it is large and deep enough to take quite large plants. Here, foxgloves and euphorbia are underplanted with violets, making an attractive early summer display.

MATERIALS AND TOOLS
Tin bath, 60 cm (24 in) wide
Gravel or similar drainage material
Equal mix loam-based soil mix and
    standard soil mix
Slow-release plant food granules
Trowel

PLANTS
3 foxgloves (*Digitalis*)
2 euphorbia
3 violets

euphorbia

foxglove

violets

1 If the bath does not have drainage holes, you should make some in the base, and then cover it with a 10 cm (4 in) layer of gravel or similar drainage material. Half-fill the bath with the soil mix, and position the foxgloves.

2 Next add the euphorbia, teasing loose the roots to enable growth if they are at all potbound. Fill between the plants with soil mix, pressing down firmly around the rootballs.

3 Finally plant the violets around the edges, where they can tumble over the sides as they grow. Water and place in a shady position.

GARDENER'S TIP

Buy your foxgloves before they have formed their flower spikes; they will transplant better and you will have the pleasure of watching them grow. Don't cut the stems down after flowering; leave them to ripen on the plant, and when you can hear the seeds rattling, simply shake them over any corner of the garden where you would like foxgloves to grow.

Plant in autumn or spring to flower in summer.

Chimney Pot Clematis

It is well known that clematis love to have their heads in the sun and their roots in the shade. A chimney pot creates the perfect environment as it provides exactly these conditions. Ideally the clematis should be planted in soil with the chimney pot placed over it, but with a little care and attention, pot-grown plants will do well for a few years.

MATERIALS AND TOOLS
Chimney pot, 60 cm (24 in) high
2 plastic pots, 20 cm (8 in) diameter
Gravel
Equal mix loam-based soil mix and
   container soil mix
Slow-release plant food granules

PLANTS
Clematis ('Prince Charles' was used
   here)

clematis

1 Fill one of the plastic pots with gravel.

2 Plant your clematis in the other plastic pot, filling around the rootball with the soil mix. Scatter a tablespoon of plant food granules over the surface of the soil mix. (The two pots will be positioned one on top of the other inside the chimney pot, as shown.)

3 Place the chimney pot over the pot of gravel and then carefully lower the clematis pot into position. It will need a sunny position and regular watering.

GARDENER'S TIP
Clematis can suffer from clematis wilt: suddenly whole stems will start to wilt and die. Cut all affected parts away from the plant and spray the remaining plant every two weeks with a product containing Benomyl.

Plant in spring to flower in summer.

Pot of Sunflowers

Sunflowers grow very well in pots provided you are not growing the giant varieties. Grow your own from seed; there are many kinds to choose from, including the double flowers used here.

MATERIALS AND TOOLS
Large glazed pot, 30 cm (12 in) diameter
Styrofoam or similar drainage material
Equal mix loam-based soil mix and container soil mix
Slow-release plant food granules

PLANTS
3 strong sunflower seedlings, approximately 20 cm (8 in) tall

sunflower seedling

1 Line the base of the pot with drainage material.

2 Fill the pot with the soil mix, pressing down so that there are no air spaces. Scoop out evenly spaced holes for each seedling and plant, firming the soil mix around the plants.

3 Scatter 1 tablespoon of plant food granules on the surface of the soil mix. Place in a sunny position, out of the wind, and water regularly.

GARDENER'S TIP

Allow at least one of the sunflower heads to set seed. As the plant starts to die back, cut off the seedhead and hang it upside-down to ripen. Reserve some seeds for next year and then hang the seedhead outside for the birds.

Plant seeds in spring and small seedlings in summer to flower in late summer.

Colorful Cooking Pot

Junk shops are a rich source of old pots and pans which can make characterful containers for plants when their kitchen days are over.

MATERIALS AND TOOLS
Cooking pot, 30 cm (12 in)
    diameter
Gravel
Equal mix loam-based soil mix and
    container soil mix
Slow-release plant food granules
Trowel

PLANTS
Ceratostigma plumbaginoides
Inula ('Oriental star' was used here)
Golden ivy

golden ivy

Ceratostigma
plumbaginoides

Inula

1 If the pot doesn't already have some holes in the base, make one or two for drainage. Fill the bottom of the pot with a 5 cm (2 in) layer of gravel.

2 Remove the *Ceratostigma* from its pot and plant it at one side of the pot.

3 Add the *Inula* and the ivy, and fill between the plants with soil mix, firming them in position as you work. Scatter a tablespoon of plant food granules over the surface of the soil mix. Water and place in a sunny position.

GARDENER'S TIP

These plants are all perennials. When the *Ceratostigma* and *Inula* have finished flowering, plant them in a border in the garden where they will flower again next year.

Plant in spring or early summer to flower in late summer.

Autumn Hanging Basket

Towards the end of summer the colors of traditional hanging baskets do not always marry happily with the reds and golds of autumn. This is the time to plant a richly colored hanging basket for winter.

MATERIALS AND TOOLS
Hanging basket, 30 cm (12 in) diameter
Plastic pot
Sphagnum moss
Equal mix loam-based soil mix and standard soil mix
Slow-release plant food granules
Trowel

PLANTS
6 winter-flowering pansies
3 variegated ivies
Euonymus fortunei ('Emerald and Gold' was used here)
2 dahlias (optional)

dahlia

winter-flowering pansy

variegated ivy

Euonymus fortunei

1 Support the hanging basket on a pot. Unhook the chain from one fixing point so that it hangs down one side of the basket. Line the base and bottom half of the basket with a generous layer of sphagnum moss.

2 Pour in soil mix until it is level with the top of the moss. Plant your first layer of three pansies and three ivies, passing the foliage through the bars of the basket, so that the rootballs of the plants are resting on the soil mix.

3 Line the rest of the basket with moss, fill up with soil mix, firming it around the roots of the ivies and pansies, and then plant the remaining plants in the top of the basket, with the *Euonymus* in the center and the pansies and dahlias surrounding it. Scatter a tablespoon of slow-release plant food granules onto the soil mix and water the hanging basket well. Re-attach the chain and hang the basket in full or partial sun.

GARDENER'S TIP

Although special hanging basket soil mixes with water-retaining gel are a boon for summer containers and hanging baskets, they can be too moist for the damper, cooler months of the year and tend to get waterlogged. Mix equal parts loam-based soil mix with a standard soil mix for good free-draining results for autumn and winter planting.

Plant in spring or summer to flower in autumn.

Heather Window Box

This is a perfect project for an absolute beginner as it is extremely simple to achieve. The bark window box is a sympathetic container for the heathers, which look very much at home in their bed of moss.

MATERIALS AND TOOLS
Bark window box, 30 cm (12 in) long
Crocks or similar drainage material
Ericaceous soil mix
Sheet moss

PLANTS
3 heathers

heathers

GARDENER'S TIP
Do not be tempted to use ordinary soil mix as it contains lime, which, with a very few exceptions, is not suitable for the majority of heathers.

Plant in autumn.

1 Put a layer of crocks or similar drainage material in the bottom of the box.

2 Remove the heathers from their pots and position them in the window box.

3 Fill the gaps between the plants with the soil mix, pressing it around the plants. Water.

4 Tuck the sheet moss snugly around the plants so that no soil is visible. Place in sun or partial sun.

Trug of Winter Pansies

Winter pansies are wonderfully resilient and will bloom bravely throughout the winter as long as they are regularly deadheaded. This trug may be moved around to provide color wherever it is needed and acts as a perfect antidote to mid-winter gloom.

MATERIALS AND TOOLS
Old wooden trug
Sphagnum moss
Standard soil mix
Slow-release plant food granules
Trowel

PLANTS
15 winter-flowering pansies

winter-flowering pansies

GARDENER'S TIP

Not everyone has an old trug available, but an old basket, colander, or an enamel bread bin could be used instead. Junk shops and flea markets are a great source of containers that are too battered for their original use, but great for planting.

Plant in autumn to flower in winter.

1 Line the trug with a generous layer of sphagnum moss.

2 Fill the moss lining with soil mix.

3 Plant the pansies by starting at one end and filling the spaces between the plants with soil mix as you go. Gently firm each plant into position and add a final layer of soil mix mixed with a tablespoon of plant food granules around the pansies. Water and place in a fairly sunny position.

Evergreen Garden

Evergreen plants come in many shapes, sizes and shades of green. Grouped together in containers they will provide you with year-round interest and color.

MATERIALS AND TOOLS
Terracotta containers of various sizes
Crocks or similar drainage material
Equal mix loam-based soil mix and
    container soil mix
Saucers
Gravel
Trowel

PLANTS
False cypress (*Chamaecyparis*)
Silver *Euonymus*
Darwin's barberry (*Berberis darwinnii*)
Barberry (*Berberis atropurpurea nana*)
Cypress (*Cupressus filifera aurea*)
Pachysandra terminalis
Bergenia

barberry

Bergenia

cypress

Pachysandra terminalis

1 Large plants, such as *Chamaecyparis*, should be potted into a proportionally large container. If it is at all potbound, tease the roots loose before planting in its new pot. Place plenty of crocks or similar drainage material at the base of the pot. Fill around the rootball with soil mix, pressing it down firmly around the edges of the pot.

2 Smaller plants, like *Bergenia*, should be planted in a pot slightly larger than its existing pot. Place crocks in the base of the pot, position the plant and then fill around the edges with soil mix.

3 Plants will stay moist longer if they are stood in saucers of wet gravel. This group of plants will do well positioned in partial shade. Water regularly and feed with slow-release plant food granules in the spring and autumn.

GARDENER'S TIP
Include some golden or variegated foliage amongst your evergreens or the group will look rather dull and one dimensional. Experiment for yourself and see how the lighter colors "lift" a group of plants.

Plant at any time of the year.

Classic Topiary

The clean lines of the topiary are matched by the simplicity of the terracotta pots. The eye is drawn to the outlines of the box plants so decorated pots would be an unneccesary distraction.

MATERIALS AND TOOLS
4 large terracotta pots
Bark mulch
Crocks
Equal mix loam-based soil mix and standard soil mix
Slow-release plant food granules
Trowel

PLANTS
4 box trees (*Buxus*) in different topiary shapes

three-ball topiary

ball topiary

corkscrew topiary

GARDENER'S TIP
Don't get carried away when you trim topiary. Little and often with an ordinary pair of scissors is better than occasional dramatic gestures with a pair of shears.

Plant at any time of the year.

1 If the plant has been well looked after in the nursery it may not need potting on yet. In this case simply slip the plant in its pot into the terracotta container.

2 To conserve moisture and conceal the plastic pot, cover with a generous layer of bark.

3 To repot a box tree, first place a good layer of crocks in the bottom of the pot.

4 Remove the tree from its plastic pot and place it in the terracotta pot. Surround the rootball with soil mix.

5 Push the soil mix down the side of the pot to ensure that there are no air spaces.

6 Scatter a tablespoon of plant food granules on the surface of the pot and then top with a good layer of bark. Water well and regularly. Position in sun or partial shade.

Gardening Practicalities

While never the most enjoyable part of gardening, feeding, weeding, watering and pest control cannot be neglected. You need not, however, spend inordinate amounts of time on these jobs since there are many short cuts and labor-saving techniques which will not compromise your plants' well-being. With these more mundane tasks under control, you will be free to enjoy your garden with peace of mind.

Left: *Evergreen shrubs and rock gardens are less demanding, but be careful not to neglect the needs of your other plants.*

Above: *Gravel is a labor-saving, and potentially attractive, alternative to the toil and trouble of maintaining a lawn.*

Seed Sowing

Some plants are very easy to sow from seed –
sunflowers rarely disappoint, even if you are a
complete beginner.

Potting-on

Sooner or later plants need repotting. Young seedlings,
shown here, don't thrive in large pots. Divide the
plants, if necessary, and plant them in pots the same
size as the one they were previously grown in.

1 Fill the pot with seed soil mix. Gently
firm and level the surface by pressing
down on the soil mix using a pot of the
same size.

2 When sowing large seeds, such as
sunflowers, use a dibber, cane or pencil to
make holes for each seed. Plant the seeds
and then firmly tap the side of the pot
with the flat of your hand to fill the holes
with soil mix. Water from above using a
fine rose on a watering can, or by standing
the pot in a saucer of water until the
surface of the soil mix is moist. Cover the
pot with a black plastic bag as most seeds
germinate best in a warm dark place.
Check daily and bring into the light when
the seedlings are showing.

1 Seedlings will probably be ready to
move into larger pots when the roots
start to emerge through the holes in the
base of the pot. To check, gently remove
the rootball from the pot and if there are
plenty of roots showing, you will know
the plants are ready for a move.

2 If there is more than one seedling in
the pot, gently break each seedling away
with a good rootball. (Some plants hate to
have their roots disturbed. The
information on the seed packet will tell
you this. These seeds are best sown
individually in peat pots.)

3 When sowing small seeds they
should be thinly scattered on the surface
of the soil mix and then covered with just
enough sieved soil mix to conceal them.
Firm the surface using another pot and
then treat in the same way as
large seeds.

3 Lower the rootball of the plant into
the pot and gently pour soil mix around it,
lightly pressing the soil mix around the
roots and stem. It doesn't matter if the
stem of the seedling is buried deeper than
it was previously as long as the leaves are
well clear of the soil. Water using a can
with a fine rose.

Planting the Border

After you have tested the soil and determined the soil type and the acid or alkaline character of it, you can decide which plants will do best in it. Although you can alter the nature of the soil, it is probably easier to opt for the plants that are known to do well in the conditions you have.

TYPES OF BORDER

The main principles to remember when designing a border are that it is a place to grow choice plants well and in harmonious combination with each other. You can create tranquil moods with pastel colors, or fire the imagination with brightly-colored flowers and angular foliage.

The bones, or structure, of the border will come from evergreen and shapely deciduous shrubs. They will provide a mass and greater interest, especially if their foliage has autumn colors. The border's ultimate form then comes from the shapes of plants. Some, low-growing and small plants with delicate flowers, will need close

WHEN TO PLANT

Traditionally, spring and autumn are considered the best times for planting, when the soil is either just warming up or still warm enough for the plants to get established. This was also the only time that field-grown plants were available to gardeners. Now with so many herbaceous plants and shrubs available as container-grown plants, the advice to plant in these two seasons is not always necessary. Provided the soil is workable, i.e. it is not frosty, waterlogged or too dry, you can plant at any time of the year.

Before planting, water the plants in their containers. If you are planting a large border, set the plants out into the positions you have chosen for them, section by section, and get an idea of how they will look. Dig planting holes large enough to take the roots comfortably and deep enough to keep the plants at the same level to which they were planted in the containers. Backfill the planting holes with the soil you have taken out. Water the plants well, swirling water and soil into the planting holes. Then firm the surface down and water regularly until the plants are well established.

PLANTING A BORDER

1 Always make sure the pots have been watered before planting, otherwise the root ball may remain dry as water runs off it when watering after planting.

2 Space the plants in their pots before you start to plant, as changes are easy at this stage. Try to visualize the plants at their final height and spread, and don't be tempted to plant them too close.

3 Knock the plant out of its pot only when you are ready to plant, so that the roots are not exposed unnecessarily to the drying air. Carefully tease out some of the roots.

4 Plant small plants with a trowel, large ones with a spade, and always work methodically from the back or from one end of the border.

5 Return the soil and make sure the plant is at its original depth or just a little deeper. Firm it with your hands or a heel to expel large pockets of air in the soil.

6 Water thoroughly unless the weather is wet. Be prepared to water regularly in dry weather for at least the first few weeks after planting.

inspection, while others, growing taller and flowering at a greater height, will rise out of the border and appear to float in bands of color above it. Each plant association should work well as an individual combination, and as a whole in the rest of the border. Look at the border as a series of small cameos and as a whole sweep of interesting plant and color combinations.

BORDER COLORS

The colors of flowers, foliage, berries and stems are perhaps the most evocative of all elements in the border. Using pale pastel colors you can create a quiet, serene effect, whereas hot vibrant colors in late summer make the opposite statement and are challenging to create. You can also make an interesting display using a restricted color palette, or even just one color. It is fun to find the plants in such a scheme that will provide you with a succession of blooms or foliage through many seasons.

If your garden is small or non-existent under the paving of a patio or balcony, do not despair: you can still grow a border by creating a mobile garden in containers. Although it will need higher maintenance than one grown directly into the soil, since you will have to provide water and nutrients for the plants, it can be an exciting, ever-changing scene.

If you plan well with seasonal changes in mind, you can create a succession of interest through the year to hold the cheery spring colors, strong summer colors, golden autumnal tones and fragrant blossom to take you through the winter.

PLANTING BULBS IN A BORDER

1 Excavate a hole large enough to take a group of bulbs and, if the soil is poor or impoverished, fork in garden compost or well-rotted manure.

3 To deter slugs and encourage good drainage around the bulbs, sprinkle more grit or coarse sand around them before returning the soil.

BULBS IN THE BORDER

Much of the color and interest in a spring border comes from flowering bulbs. Daffodils, tulips, snowdrops, bluebells, crocuses, *Iris reticulata, Cyclamen coum,* aconites, dog's tooth lilies, and hyacinths can be used "en masse" in borders or singly under trees, or – for daffodils, crocuses, bluebells and aconites – naturalized in lawns.

2 Space out the bulbs, planting at a depth that will leave them covered with about twice their own depth of soil.

4 If planting summer-flowering bulbs in spring, position with small canes so that you do not accidentally hoe or cultivate the area before the shoots come up.

Plant spring-flowering bulbs, except tulips, from late August through to November so that they have a long growing season in the ground and can establish well before the cold of winter sets in. Plant tulips later, from October through to November. Plant the bulbs in layers or decks, with late-flowering varieties deeper into the ground, and early-flowering bulbs nearer

Above: *Crocuses show the true versatility of bulbs. They can be used in beds and borders to bring pockets of color when there is not much else out, and can even be naturalized in the lawn.*

the surface. In this way, you achieve a simple succession of flowering bulbs without too much disturbance of the soil. Summer-flowering bulbs such as lilies, alliums, nerines and galtonia extend the season and continue to provide interest in early and late summer.

When bulb flowers are spent, take off the flower heads, but allow the foliage to die down

DIVIDING OVERCROWDED CLUMPS

1 If a large clump of established bulbs, such as daffodils, begins to flower poorly, overcrowding may be the cause. Lift, divide and replant. You can do this when the plants are dormant, but if you do it before the leaves die down completely it is easier to see where the clumps are.

2 Separate the clump into smaller pieces, and replant some of the large, healthy bulbs in the same place. Either discard or give away the surplus bulbs if you have too many, or replant them elsewhere.

naturally. In a border, this can make for unsightly, untidy effects, but by using raffia you can loosely tie the foliage together, but do not waste time and effort bending it over. When the foliage turns yellow, usually after about six weeks, cut it back to the ground and leave the bulbs undisturbed. If the bulbs are not hardy, such as some summer-flowering varieties, lift them and clean and dry them off before storing them for planting again next spring. Tulips should be lifted as well and stored as they are attacked by pests and disease if left in the ground during the summer.

Every two or three years it is worthwhile to lift and divide large, established clumps of bulbs. Overcrowding may reduce their flowering vigor and by dividing and replanting, you will renew their flowering capacity. You will not be able to replant all the bulbs in the same position and therefore you will need to find additional space elsewhere in the garden.

THE GARDEN AS A HABITAT

Get to know the site and soil in different parts of your garden, and plant them with the right plants for that particular habitat, as if they were outside the manipulated garden and growing where they were best suited in a natural situation. To do this well, you have to know a little about the plants you want to grow. The conditions they need are an indication of the habitats they originally came from. Epimediums, for example, with their delicate spring foliage, good autumn color and small, but interesting flowers, suit the shadier areas of a border, a clue to their woodland edge origins.

Above: *Hostas have been planted at the front of this mixed border. The height differential gives you the benefit of two borders.*

SHRUBS IN THE BORDER

Shrubs, such as *Choisya ternata* 'Sundance', deutzia and weigela, offer bursts of foliage and flower color that are substantial for long periods during the year, unlike some herbaceous border plants. They act as a framework, as their shapes are stronger and more pronounced, and they add height, shape, foliage and floral interest, as well as providing a variation of rhythm to the whole of the border.

ROSES IN THE BORDER

Old shrub roses, including damask, centifolia, gallica, musk, and alba, bourbon, hybrid perpetual and portland roses, make a romantic and soft addition to the border. Although they are often described as needing little attention, like most plants they respond well to care given at the right time to prevent problems later. You must remember to remove their

dead or damaged wood in spring, and you should also mulch and fertilize them well in spring. If they are growing in a border where they have to compete with other plants, make sure they are well watered throughout the dry seasons. If they need spraying against black or green aphids, use a beneficial insect-friendly spray, and only use it on calm windless days, when the roses are in shade. Deadhead when the blooms are spent, unless the rose is also grown for its autumn hips, in which case, leave the spent flowers in place.

Modern roses, specially bred as carpet or ground cover plants, are also highly useful in sloping borders or on banks, if you want to make a good floral effect. Often their foliage is attractive too, which extends their usefulness. They will also help to maintain the border, by suppressing weeds.

Sheet Mulches

Mulches fall into two main groups: the mainly inorganic ones made from various forms of plastic or rubber sheets, and loose ones such as garden compost and chipped bark that will eventually rot down and add to the humus content of the soil.

"Loose" mulches are described on pages 164–65. Both have their uses, and you may want to add one of the more decorative loose mulches to make a sheet mulch visually more acceptable. This can be more cost-effective than using a loose mulch alone, which has to be applied at least 2 in thick to be an effective weed control.

MULCHING WITH A SHEET
Use this method for low-maintenance shrub beds and newly planted trees.

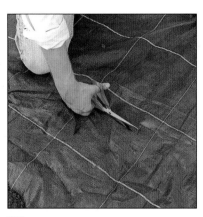

1 Sheet mulches are most useful in shrub beds that can be left undisturbed for some years, and are best used when the bed or border is newly planted. Always prepare the ground as thoroughly as you would if not using a mulching sheet.

Make a slit around the edge of the bed with a spade, and push the sheet into this. For a vegetable plot you can use special plastic pegs, but these are too conspicuous for an ornamental position.

2 Make cross-shaped planting slits in the sheet with a knife or scissors. If planting a shrub you will probably have to make slits large enough to take a spade for planting. This won't matter as the sheet can be folded back into place.

3 Small plants can be planted with a trowel, but for shrubs you will need to use a spade. Provided the ground has been well prepared before the sheet was laid, it should be easy to dig out the planting hole.

4 Sheet mulches are very useful around newly planted trees and shrubs. The best way to apply the sheet is to cut a square or circle to size, then make a single slit from the center. Place it around the tree or shrub – and the stake if there is one – and simply fold it back into place. It won't matter if the join is not perfect as you can hide it with a decorative mulch.

5 Although most of the sheet mulch will be hidden as the plants grow, it will be very conspicuous initially. A layer of a decorative mulch such as chipped bark or gravel will make it much more acceptable.

Black polyethylene is inexpensive and widely available. It does not allow water to penetrate, so it's best used in narrow strips, alongside a hedge.

Although more expensive than polyethylene sheets, woven plastic mulches allow water to seep through while keeping out light.

Butyl rubber is a very long-lasting waterproof mulch. It is expensive, but you only require a thin gauge. It is more suitable for the area immediately around trees than as cover for a large area.

Some sheet mulches are made from degradable materials such as wood waste. This is a good option if you want a sheet mulch that will eventually disappear as it rots.

Below: *Established plants are more difficult to mulch with a sheet, but trees and hedges can be mulched this way very satisfactorily. If you want to control weeds along a young hedge, lay black polyethylene in two strips, one on either side of the hedge.*

PRACTICAL POINTS

- Always prepare the soil thoroughly before laying the sheet.

- Enrich the soil with plenty of organic material such as rotted manure or garden compost – you won't have an opportunity later.

- Add fertilizer and water it in thoroughly – only liquid feeds are practical once the sheet is in position.

- Soak the ground before applying the sheet.

Above: *Sheet mulches can look unattractive in the ornamental garden. They are better covered with a shallow layer of a decorative mulch too.*

Loose Mulches

Most loose mulches are visually more acceptable, and the organic ones gradually rot or become integrated into the soil by insect life and worm activity, thus helping to improve soil structure and fertility.

Loose mulches have to be thick to suppress weeds well. Aim for a thickness of about 2 in.

APPLYING A LOOSE MULCH

1 Prepare the ground thoroughly, digging it over and working in plenty of organic material such as rotted manure or garden compost if the soil is impoverished.

2 Loose mulches will control annual weeds and prevent new perennial ones getting a foothold. You must dig up deep-rooted perennial weeds, otherwise they could grow through the mulch.

3 Water the ground thoroughly before applying the mulch. Do not apply a mulch to dry ground.

4 Spread the mulch thickly. This is bark mulch, but there are many other decorative mulches that you could choose from.

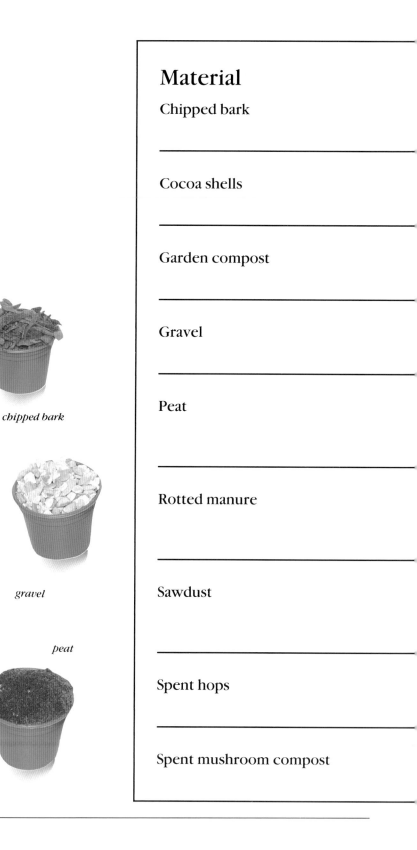

chipped bark

gravel

peat

Material

Chipped bark

Cocoa shells

Garden compost

Gravel

Peat

Rotted manure

Sawdust

Spent hops

Spent mushroom compost

Advantages	Disadvantages
Very ornamental, and lasts for a long time before it needs replacing	Can be relatively expensive. May take some nitrogen from the soil as it rots down
Light to handle. Attractive color and pleasant smell when handling. Lasts for a long time	Can be relatively expensive. Sometimes can encourage growth of superficial molds
Excellent soil conditioner. High level of nutrients. Free if you make your own	Soon breaks down, which enriches the soil but means you need to keep freshening. Not visually attractive
Visually pleasing. Long-lasting	Contains no nutrients. Individual pieces may be a problem if they get onto the lawn
Visually pleasing and pleasant to handle. Very useful for plants that require acid conditions	Relatively expensive. Low in nutrients. Many people prefer to avoid its use because its extraction depletes peat reserves and peat bog habitats
Excellent soil conditioner. Useful nutrient levels. Can be inexpensive if you have a local source	Soon breaks down, which enriches the soil but means you need to keep freshening. Not visually attractive, and can smell if not thoroughly rotted
Usually cheap if you have access to a plentiful supply. Usually slow to decay	Can temporarily deplete the soil of nitrogen when rotting down. Can be visually pleasing when newly applied but soon looks unattractive
Usually quite inexpensive if you live in an area where they are readily available. Easy and pleasant to handle	Can be difficult to obtain, especially in small quantities
Usually relatively inexpensive. Should contain animal manure and straw, which will improve the soil	Normally contains lime, so should be avoided on alkaline soils or where acid-loving plants are grown

Controlling Weeds

The only place where weeds are acceptable is in a wildlife corner, although some people find daisies in the lawn a very attractive feature. Generally, however, weeds have to be controlled, and pulling them up by hand is a tedious and time-consuming job that few of us enjoy. It's even more frustrating if they grow again within days.

There are two main weapons if you want to cut down on weeding: mulching, which uses no chemicals, and herbicides – or weedkillers if you prefer to use a more descriptive term!

KILLING WEEDS IN BEDS AND BORDERS

Although there are weedkillers that will kill some problem grasses growing among broad-leaved plants, generally you can't use selective weedkillers in beds and borders. Most weedkillers will kill or damage whatever they come into contact with, but there are ways in which you can use herbicides around ornamental plants to minimize the amount of hand weeding necessary.

2 You may be able to treat areas in a shrub border with a watered-on weedkiller simply by shielding the cultivated plants. If deep-rooted perennials are not a problem you can use a contact weedkiller that will act rather like a chemical hoe (a real hoe may be an easier alternative to mixing and applying a weedkiller if the area is small).

1 Deep-rooted perennial "problem" weeds, such as bindweed, are best treated by painting on a translocated weedkiller such as one based on glyphosate. Ordinary contact weedkillers may not kill all the roots, but this chemical is moved by the plant to all parts. Even so you may have to treat really difficult weeds a number of times. Use a gel formulation to paint on where watering on the weedkillers may cause damage to adjacent ornamentals.

3 Once the ground is clear, if you don't want to use a mulch, try applying a weedkiller intended to prevent new weed seedlings emerging. These are only suitable for certain shrubs and fruit crops, but they remain near the surface above root level and only act on seedlings that try to germinate. These should suppress most new weeds for many months.

WEED-FREE PATHS

Paths can easily be kept weed-free for a season using one of the products sold for the purpose. Most of these contain a cocktail of chemicals, some of which act quickly to kill existing weeds and others that prevent the growth of new ones for many months. A single application will keep the path clear for a long time.

Use an improvised shield to prevent the weedkiller being blown onto the flowerbeds.

WORDS OF WARNING

Weedkillers are extremely useful aids, but they can be disastrous if you use the wrong ones, or are careless in their application.

- Always check to see whether it is a total or selective weedkiller.

- If selective, make sure it will kill your problem weeds – and make sure it is suitable for applying to the area you have in mind. Lawn weedkillers should be used only on lawns.

- Don't apply liquid weedkillers on a windy day.

- For greater control, use a dribble bar rather than an ordinary rose on your watering-can.

- Keep a special watering-can for weedkillers, otherwise residues may harm your plants.

- Avoid run-off onto flower beds, and if necessary use a shield while applying a weedkiller.

Right: *Paths can be marred by weeds. Either make sure they are mortared between the joints, or use a path weedkiller to keep them looking ship shape.*

Weed-free Lawns

A weedy lawn will mar your garden, but with modern weedkillers, it's quite easy to eliminate weeds to leave your grass looking like a lawn rather than a mown wildflower meadow.

KILLING WEEDS IN LAWNS

This method ensures a weed-free lawn with as little as one application a year.

Above: *A lawn like this is the result of regular weeding and feeding. Once weeds have been eliminated, however, the grass should hold its own against new weeds.*

1 Weeds in lawns are best controlled by a selective hormone weedkiller, ideally applied in mid- or late spring. These are usually applied as a liquid, using a dribble bar attached to a watering-can. To ensure even application you should mark out lines with string, spacing them the width of the dribble bar apart.

2 Always mix and apply the weedkiller as recommended by the manufacturer. There are a number of different plant hormones used, some killing certain weeds better than others, so always check that it is recommended for the weeds you most want to control. When mixed, simply walk along each strip slowly enough for the droplets from the dribble bar to cover the area evenly.

3 If your lawn also needs feeding, you can save time by using a combined weed and feed. The most efficient way to apply these – which are likely to be granular rather than liquid – is with a fertilizer spreader.

4 If you have just a few troublesome weeds in a small area, it is a waste of time and money treating the whole lawn. For this job a spot weeder that you dab or wipe onto the offending weed will work well.

Above: *A weed-free lawn leads the eye to a distant patio.*

Right: *The few weeds in this lawn are probably not worth worrying about, but you can easily spot treat an area if you don't want to waste time treating the whole lawn.*

DEALING WITH MOSS

Moss is much more difficult to control than ordinary lawn weeds, and hand weeding is simply not a practical option. Use a moss-killer – some you water on; others are sprinkled on. Ask your garden center for advice about which is best for your circumstances.

Once the moss has been killed, it is worth trying to avoid the conditions that encourage it: shade and poor drainage.

Feeding

Feeding really does pay dividends. If you see a garden with particularly lush and healthy-looking plants, the chances are they have been well fed.

Feeding used to be a job that had to be tackled several times during the course of a season, and some enthusiasts still feed their plants once a week or even more frequently. If you use modern slow-release and controlled-release fertilizers, however, feeding is something you can do just a couple of times a year.

Liquid feeds, nevertheless, are more instant in effect and still have a use, being invaluable when plants need a quick pick-me-up.

FEEDING CONTAINERS

Container plants require supplementary nutrients to keep them in good health.

2 If you find it more convenient, you can place sachets of slow-release fertilizer beneath the plants when you plant them.

1 A controlled- or slow-release fertilizer added to the potting soil at planting time will keep most containers blooming well all summer. Follow the instructions for application rates.

*slow-release
fertilizer granules*

*slow-release
fertilizer pellets*

*slow-release
fertilizer sachet*

SLOW- AND CONTROLLED-RELEASE

Some fertilizers are described as slow-release and controlled-release. Both allow the nutrients to seep out into the soil over a period of months, but controlled-release fertilizers are affected by soil temperature. Nutrients are only released when the soil is warm enough for growth in most plants.

3 If you can buy pellets of slow-release fertilizer like this, place them beneath individual plants at planting time.

FEEDING THE LAWN

There are several ways to do this, all taking relatively little time.

1 The quickest way to feed your lawn is with a wheeled spreader like this. Although individual models vary, you can usually adjust the delivery rate. Test the rate on a measured area of path first, then sweep up the fertilizer and weigh it to make sure the application rate is right.

2 An easy way to give your lawn a liquid boost is to use a sprinkler system into which you can introduce special fertilizer pellets. It will feed the lawn as it waters, and you don't have to stand there holding the hose.

3 A hose-end sprayer like this is a good way to apply a soluble fertilizer for a quick response. It is much quicker than mixing it in watering-cans to apply. You can use this type of hose-end sprayer for beds and borders as well as for the lawn.

BEDS AND BORDERS

An annual feed will keep even the most demanding plants happy.

1 Most established plants, but especially demanding ones such as roses, benefit from annual feeding. Apply a slow- or controlled-release fertilizer in spring or early summer, sprinkling it around the bushes. Keep it away from the stem, sprinkling it further out where most of the active root growth is.

2 Hoe it into the surface so that it penetrates the root area more quickly.

3 Unless rain is expected, water it in. This will make the fertilizer active more quickly in dry conditions.

soluble fertilizer

Common Pests

Vine weevils *(above)*
These white grubs are a real problem. The first sign of an infestation is the sudden collapse of the plant, which has died as a result of the weevil eating its roots. Systemic insecticides or natural predators can be used as a preventative, but once a plant has been attacked it is usually too late. Never re-use the soil from an affected plant.

Caterpillars *(above)*
The occasional caterpillar can be simply picked off the plant and disposed of as you see fit, but a major infestation can strip a plant before your eyes. Contact insecticides are usually very effective in these cases.

Slugs and snails
As a preventative measure, smear a circle of petroleum jelly below the rim of the pot as the slugs and snails will not cross this. If there is already a problem with slugs in the pot, slug pellets should deal with any resident pests.

Scale insects
These can be very troublesome on container-grown plants, particularly on those with waxy leaves, such as bay, citrus, *Ficus* and *Stephanotis*. The first sign is often a sticky substance on the leaves. If you look under the leaves and at the leaf joints you may be able to spot the scales. A serious infestation will be indicated by a black sooty mold. The scale insect's waxy coating makes it resistant to contact insecticides, so use of a systemic insecticide is essential. As scale insects develop over quite a long period it is important to treat regularly for a couple of months.

Whitefly *(above)*
As their name indicates, these are tiny white flies which flutter in clouds when disturbed from their feeding places on the undersides of leaves. Whitefly are particularly troublesome in conservatories where a dry atmosphere will encourage them to breed. Keep the air as moist as possible. Contact insecticides will need more than one application to deal with an infestation, but a systemic insecticide will protect the plant for weeks.

Insecticides

There are two main types of insecticide available to combat common pests.

Contact insecticides
These must be sprayed directly onto the insects to be effective. Most organic insecticides work this way, but they generally kill all insects, even beneficial ones such as dragon flies and ladybugs. Try to remove these before spraying the infected plant.

Mealy bugs
These look like spots of white mold. Like scale insects they are hard to shift and regular treatment with a systemic insecticide is the best solution.

Aphids
One of the most common plant pests. These green sap-sucking insects feed on the tender growing tips of plants. Most insecticides are effective against aphids. Choose one that will not harm ladybugs as aphids are a favorite food of theirs.

Red Spider mite (*above*)
This is another insect that thrives indoors in dry conditions. Constant humidity will reduce the chance of an infestation. The spider mite is barely visible to the human eye, but infestation is indicated by the presence of fine webs and mottling of the plant's leaves. To treat an infestation, it is best to move the plant outdoors if the weather is suitable, spray with an insecticide and allow the plant time to recover before bringing it back indoors.

Systemic insecticides
These work by being absorbed by the plant's root or leaf system and killing the insects that come into contact with the plant. This will work for difficult pests such as vine weevils which are hidden in the soil, and scale insects, which protect themselves from above with a scaly cover.

BIOLOGICAL CONTROL
Commercial growers now use biological control in their greenhouses, which means natural predators are introduced to eat the pest population. Although not all are suitable for the amateur gardener, they can be used in conservatories for dealing with pests such as whitefly.

Automatic Watering

An automatic watering system will save you a lot of time and is better for the plants, which are less likely to suffer from water stress. Some hoses, sprinklers and timing devices are described on the following pages, but these are just some of the systems that you can buy. Look at garden centers and in magazine advertisements to see which appear to be the most appropriate for your needs.

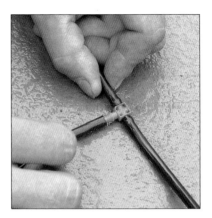

PLANNING THE SYSTEM

Work out the layout of your self-watering system first, and decide the number and kind of delivery devices (such as drip heads) you need. Kits are a useful start, but are unlikely to contain the exact number of components that you need. Check that the master unit or flow-reducer will support the number of drips required.

Above: *Most automatic watering systems are fitted with a suitable control system to reduce the pressure, and act as a filter. Designs vary, and either screw onto the outside tap or are inserted into the hose system. If the tap does not have a non-return valve fitted to prevent back-siphonage, make sure the master unit has one.*

Above: *Drip-feed systems are versatile enough to be used for plants in beds, borders or in containers. Use a T-joint to run branches or tubes for individual drip heads.*

Above: *Some automatic systems are controlled by the moisture level in the soil, but most operate on a continuous drip basis. Even if you can control the drip rate, too much water may be delivered if operated continuously. A timing device will turn your watering system on and off automatically, yet can easily be deactivated if the weather is bad. This one, operated by a battery, can be set to water your garden up to six times a day.*

Above: *Unless your garden is extremely small, it's best to install a pipeline buried just beneath the ground surface, then you can "plug in" various watering devices as necessary. With this particular system a sprinkler can simply be pushed onto the fitting set flush with the lawn or soil surface.*

Above: *Push the head onto the hose, and if necessary hold the delivery tube in position with a pipe peg. If the rate of delivery can be adjusted, the instructions that come with the kit will explain how this is done.*

Right: *An automatic watering device will keep your garden lush throughout the summer.*

Watering Aids

You may find the choice of watering aids bewildering, but decide what you want to water, then choose the kind of fitting that will do the job. You can avoid watering altogether if you choose drought-resistant plants, abandon containers, and don't mind a brown lawn in a dry summer. However, if you want lush, green grass and lots of colorful containers without the sometimes twice-daily chore of watering, some kind of automatic watering system is essential in the low-maintenance garden.

Above: *This type of drip feed is left connected continuously, through a flow-reducer provided, and the water-filled ceramic cone detects whether the soil is moist enough. Dry soil creates a partial vacuum, which then allows water to flow through the thin tubing, and the rate of flow can be adjusted. This system can be used in beds and borders but is ideal for troughs, tubs, and window-boxes. Like many drip systems, this one can also be fed from a reservoir or tank instead of being connected to the main water supply.*

Above: *A drip-feed system is ideal for hanging baskets and window-boxes. Watering will probably have to be programmed to operate a couple of times a day – even in wet weather containers often need additional water because of the "rain shadow" created by the walls.*

Left: *Leaky-pipe and perforated hose systems are suitable for beds and borders or the kitchen garden. The special hoses are either porous or have many very fine holes, and water gradually seeps through them. You can bury them beneath the surface or lay them on top of the soil (useful where you might want to move the hose around).*

Watering

Too much water is as bad as too little – get the balance right and let your plants thrive.

1 The best way to avoid overwatering a plant is to stand the pot in a saucer and water into the saucer. The plant's roots can then take up moisture as needed.

2 Most plants are quite happy to be watered from above, as here. This is not recommended for plants with velvety leaves such as African violets. They should be watered in the saucer.

3 Houseplants enjoy being sprayed with water, but in hard water areas you should use rain water or bottled water.

Water-retaining gel

One of the main problems for most container gardeners is the amount of watering required to keep the plants thriving. Adding water-retaining gels to soil mixes will certainly help reduce this task. Sachets of gel are available from garden centers.

1 Pour the recommended amount of water into a bowl.

2 Scatter the gel over the surface, stirring occasionally until it has absorbed the water.

3 Add to your soil mix at the recommended rate.

4 Mix the gel in thoroughly before using it for planting.

THE GOOD PLANT GUIDE

Although – as this book shows – effective planning and well-designed hard-landscaping are vital in creating a garden, it is of course the plants you choose which will ultimately determine its overall look. It is impossible to give many planting suggestions for beds and borders in a book of this size, and in any case you should try to include mainly those plants that appeal to you rather than follow another person's preferences.

Most garden centers now have well-labeled plants, often with a picture of the mature plant as well as notes about its height, spread, soil preferences and aspect it prefers, and a good plant encyclopedia will fill in most of the gaps.

The vast majority of plants will grow well in most gardens, tolerating a wide pH range (a measure of how acid or alkaline the soil is), and doing well in sun or partial shade. It is only where your soil is extreme in some way, or the aspect particularly unfavorable (very shady, exposed and windy, or very acid or alkaline, for example), that you will have to consider whether the plant will thrive.

This section of the book tells you which plants should be suitable for a range of problem sites, so you know which ones to consider when you browse through catalogs or go around the garden centers.

There are also suggestions for other groups of plants for which ideas are usually welcome, such as those that make a good focal point, and plants to grow for wildlife, or for fragrance.

Bear in mind that these short lists are only a selection of the many plants that may be appropriate. But they are all dependable plants, and are well worth including as, at least, a starting point.

Focal Point Plants

The majority of these plants look good in borders, but most of them are particularly striking as individual specimens, or in a position where they stand out above the rest of the plants in the border. They are plants that will catch the eye, even from a distance, and in many cases serve a similar purpose to a garden ornament.

BORDER PERENNIALS

Acanthus spinosissimus (bear's-breech)
Above: Large, spiny-looking leaves, topped by 4-foot spikes of purple and white flowers in summer.

Agapanthus hybrids (Lily-of-the Nile)
Above: Large, rounded heads of blue flowers on stiff stems about 2–2½ feet tall.

Allium giganteum (giant onion)
Ball-like heads about 4 inches across containing masses of small, mauve flowers on stiff stems about 4 feet tall.

Crambe cordifolia (colewort)
Above: Huge, dark green leaves and cloud-like masses of small, white flowers in early summer on stems about 6 feet tall.

Eremurus robustus (giant desert-candle)
Above: Tall flower spikes often 8 feet tall in late spring and early summer. Peach-colored flowers.

Gunnera manicata
Enormous leaves like a giant rhubarb, on plants up to 10 feet tall. It requires very moist soil.

Kniphofia (red hot poker)
Above: Stiff, blade-like leaves and poker-like spikes of usually red and yellow flowers, 3–6 feet tall.

Phormium tenax (New Zealand flax)
Above: Clumps of broad, strap-like green, purple or variegated, according to species or variety; most are 3–6 feet tall.

GRASSES

Arundo donax (giant reed)
A large grass, up to 8 feet with long, drooping, blue-green leaves. "Variegatus," banded white, is only about half this height.

Cortaderia selloana (pampas grass)
Above: Large grass with 6-foot long, silvery white flower plumes in fall. Evergreen. For a small garden use "Pumila" – 4 feet.

SHRUBS AND TREES

Cordyline australis (cabbage tree)
Above: Palm that is hardy except in cold areas. Strap-shaped leaves (on tall stems on mature plants). Can reach tree-like size.

Fatsia japonica
(Japan fatsia)
Above: Hand-shaped, large, glossy green leaves. White, ball-shaped flower head in fall on mature plants. 6 feet or more tall.

Garrya elliptica (silk-tassel)
Evergreen of undistinguished appearance most of year, but spectacular long catkins in winter.

Mahonia "Charity"
Evergreen with stiff, upright growth and large, divided leaves. Sprays of yellow flowers in winter. Grows up 8 feet or more.

Paulownia tomentosa (coppiced)
If pruned to just above ground level each spring, this tree can be grown as a tall shrub with leaves 2 feet or more across.

Trachycarpus fortunei
(windmill palm)
Above: Clusters of large, fan-shaped leaves on a tall stem. Only hardy in areas where winters are mild.

Yucca gloriosa (and *Y. filamentosa*)
Above: Stiff, sword-like evergreen leaves (on a stout stem in the case of *Y. gloriosa*), with imposing spike of creamy-white bells.

Plants for Shady Areas

Shade-tolerant plants are among the most useful in the garden as they can make the most of those unpromising areas that are usually dull and uninteresting. A few well-chosen, attractive shade plants can transform those parts of the garden that receive little direct sun into a lush and lovely area that you will want to visit.

BORDER PERENNIALS FOR DRY SHADE

Anemone japonica (*A.* x *hybrida*)
White or pink, single or double flowers about 2 inches across in late summer and fall, on stems 3–4 feet tall.

Bergenia
Above: Large, rounded, glossy leathery leaves (sometimes purplish in winter). Flowers – mostly pink – in spring. 1–1½ feet.

Brunnera macrophylla
Loose heads of blue, forget-me-not-like flowers in spring, but taller at about 1½ feet. Avoid dry soil.

Euphorbia (spurge)
There are many kinds, but for shade look for *E. amygdaloides*, *E. griffithii* and *E. robbiae* (one of the best for shade).

Liriope muscari (big blue lily-turf)
Grass-like tufts of foliage, with spikes of blue, bead-like flowers in fall. 1–1½ feet.

Pulmonaria (lungwort)
There are many species and varieties, most with silver-splashed leaves. The spring flowers are in shades of blue and pink.

BORDER PERENNIALS FOR MOIST SHADE

Astilbe hybrids
Above: Deeply cut foliage, topped with plumes of pink, red or white summer flowers. 2–2½ feet.

Astrantia (masterwort)
White to pink flowers with papery bracts, on slender stems, in summer. 2-2½ feet.

Dicentra spectabilis (bleeding heart)
Fern-like foliage, topped by arching sprays of pendulous pink or white flowers in spring. 2 feet.

Helleborus (hellebore)
The most popular species are *H. niger* (winter) and *H. orientalis* (spring), but there are other species and hybrids to try.

Hosta (plantain-lily)
These popular foliage plants come in many variations, so choose species or varieties with leaves that particularly appeal to you.

Rodgersia (Rodger's-flower)
Large, bold, divided or lobed leaves (there are several species) and plumes of white or pink flowers in summer. 3–5 feet.

SHRUBS FOR DRY SHADE

Aucuba japonica (Japanese aucuba)
Above: Large, glossy evergreen leaves, splashed yellow or gold. Flowers inconspicuous, occasionally red berries. 5 feet.

Ilex (holly)
There are dozens of excellent hollies, many attractively variegated. If you want berries, check that you are buying a female variety.

Mahonia
There are many species and hybrids, all with large, divided leaves and yellow flowers in winter or spring.

Pachysandra terminalis
A low-growing ground cover about 1 foot tall, with white, inconspicuous flowers. "Variegata" is a more attractive plant.

Skimmia
Glossy leaved evergreens, with red berries (if you buy a female variety or one that has flowers of both sexes). About 3 feet.

Vinca (periwinkle)
A rather untidy, spreading ground cover, but useful for its usually blue flowers all summer long. There are variegated forms.

SHRUBS FOR MOIST SHADE

Camellia
Above: Large flowers in spring, set against glossy, evergreen leaves. There are many different kinds.

Fatsia japonica (Japan fatsia)
A bold foliage plant with large, hand-shaped leaves. Grows to about 6 feet.

Hamamelis mollis (witch-hazel)
A large shrub to 10 feet or more, grown for its spidery-looking, yellow, fragrant flowers in winter.

Rhododendron
Popular flowering woodland plants. There are hundreds of widely available varieties to choose from.

Sarcococca
Glossy, evergreen foliage and white, winter flowers that are small but very fragrant. About 3 feet.

Viburnum davidii
Low-growing evergreen with conspicuously veined leathery leaves. Turquoise fruits on female plants.

Plants for Sunny and Dry Areas

Few plants object to sunshine, but the dry soil that sometimes goes with a shallow or sandy soil in a sun-baked situation is a more demanding environment. For a position like this, choose plants that are naturally adapted to such conditions and will thrive in them.

SHRUBS

Caryopteris x *clandonensis* (hybrid bluebeard)
Clusters of bright blue flowers in late summer and early fall. Gray, aromatic leaves. Height about 3 feet.

Cistus (sun-rose)
Above: Large, single flowers between late spring and midsummer. Mainly pinks and white, and often blotched. 1½–3 feet.

Convolvulus cneorum
A leafy evergreen with a silvery appearance. Funnel-shaped, white flowers in summer, on a plant that grows to about 2 feet.

Cytisus (broom)
There are many species and hybrids to choose from, mainly with bright, pea-type flowers.

Helianthemum nummularium (common rock-rose)
Above: Low-growing shrubs to about 1 foot, with masses of single or double pink, red, yellow or white flowers in early summer.

Santolina chamaecyparissus (lavender cotton)
Finely divided, stem-hugging gray leaves that create a silvery mound about 2 foot tall. Button-like, yellow flowers in summer.

Senecio
S. greyi and *S.* 'Sunshine' *(above)* are similar plants with gray leaves on bushy plants about 3 feet tall. Yellow daisy flowers in summer.

Yucca
Any of the hardy yuccas make imposing plants, with spiky leaves and bold spikes of white, bell-like flowers in summer.

BORDER PERENNIALS

Achillea filipendulina (fernleaf yarrow)
Above: Flat, yellow flower heads over fern-like foliage, flowes between early summer and mid-fall.

Agapanthus (Lily-of-the-Nile)
Large, rounded heads of blue or white flowers on stiff stems about 2–2½ feet tall. Not suitable for cold winter areas.

Echinops ritro (small globe thistle)
Above: Globular, steely-blue flower heads in mid- and late summer, on plants about 3 feet tall with gray-green, deeply lobed leaves.

Geranium (cranesbill)
Above: There are many species of these summer-flowering border plants, with pink or blue flowers, most 1–2 feet tall.

Iris germanica hybrids (bearded)
The border bearded irises, which flower in early summer, come in many colors. Most grow to about 2–3 feet tall.

Kniphofia hybrids (red hot poker)
Stiff, blade-like leaves and imposing poker-like spikes of usually red and yellow flowers. 3–6 feet tall.

Nepeta mussinii (*N.* x *faassenii*) (catmint)
Above: Massed spikes of blue flowers in summer, backed by gray-green leaves. Grows up to 1–2 feet according to variety.

Verbascum (mullein)
There are several good hybrids for the border, but they tend to be short-lived. Tall spikes of pink, yellow or white flowers.

Plants for Chalky Soil

Alkaline soils – predominantly those that are in chalky areas – pose a problem for many plants. The high pH (alkalinity) can cause various nutrients and trace elements to become locked into a form unavailable to the plants, which then grow poorly and often have yellowing leaves. You can overcome some of these problems with cultural techniques and the use of special chemicals, but it is easier to concentrate on those plants that grow well on chalky soils.

SHRUBS

Buddleia davidii (butterfly-bush)
Annual pruning insures sprays of white, mauve or purple flowers on bushes about 6 feet tall.

Clematis
Above and top: There are many species and hybrids of these popular climbers to be grown, all of which should thrive on chalky soils.

Cotoneaster
Choose from the many kinds of cotoneaster, deciduous or evergreen, ground-huggers or tall shrubs. All tolerate chalky soil.

Helianthemum nummularium (common rock-rose)
Low-growing shrubs to about 1 foot, with masses of single or double pink, red, yellow or white flowers in early summer.

Lavandula (lavender)
Above: Lavender, blue, pink or white flowers between mid-summer and early fall. Usually gray-green, aromatic foliage.

Paeonia suffruticosa (tree peony)
Above: Very large flowers – 6 inches across – in shades of pink or red, as well as white, in late spring. 5–6 feet.

Pyracantha (firethorn)
Small, white flowers in early summer, followed by red, orange or yellow berries. Grow against a wall or freestanding.

Syringa (lilac)
Above: *S. vulgaris* (common lilac) and other species of these popular and fragrant shrubs will all thrive on chalky soils.

BORDER PERENNIALS

Dianthus (carnations, pinks)
Above: Border carnations and pinks of all kinds will do well on chalky soils. Your garden center should have a good selection.

Doronicum (leopardsbane)
Above: Bright yellow, single, daisy-type flowers, or doubles, in late spring and early summer. Most grow to about 2 feet.

Gypsophila paniculata (baby's-breath)
Masses of small white or pink flowers in summer, on a loose plant to about 3 feet. The lax stems benefit from a support.

Helleborus
The most popular species are *H. niger* (winter) and *H. orientalis* (spring), but there are other species and hybrids to try.

Paeonia (peony)
Above: Large single or double flowers about 5 inces across, in late spring or early summer, mainly pinks and reds. 2–2½ feet.

Scabiosa (scabious)
Above: *S. caucasica* (blue flowers from summer to fall) is the popular border species, but other scabious will also thrive on chalk.

Verbascum (mullein)
There are several good hybrids for the border, but they tend to be short-lived. Tall spikes of pink, yellow or white flowers.

Plants for Acid Soil

Acid soils are generally less of a problem than alkaline ones. Most plants that tolerate a wide range of soil will do well on reasonably acid soils, especially if you add lime to neutralize the effect. The plants listed here not only thrive in acid soils but are also particularly reluctant to grow in alkaline conditions – so also use this list as an indication of what to avoid for chalky soils.

SHRUBS

Azalea
Above: There are evergreen and semi-evergreen azaleas, ranging in size from dwarfs for the rock garden to large woodland plants.

Calluna vulgaris (heather)
There are hundreds of varieties, some grown for foliage color. Most flower late summer and fall. 1–1½ feet.

Camellia
Above: Large, rose-like flowers in spring, set against evergreen leaves. There are many different kinds.

Corylopsis pauciflora (buttercup winter hazel)
Spreading growth and slender branches with pale yellow catkin flowers. Grows to about 6 feet.

Daboecia cantabrica (Irish heath)
Above: Heather-like plant with pink or white bell-like flowers on bushy plants about 2 feet tall. Flowers from summer to fall.

Gaultheria procumbens (wintergreen)
Above: A creeping plant with small evergreen leaves, useful for ground cover. Grown mainly for its red berries. 6 inches.

Halesia carolina (Caroline silverbell)
A large, spreading shrub growing to more than 10 feet. Bell-shaped white flowers appear in late spring.

Kalmia latifolia (mountain-laurel)
Above: Evergreen with glossy green leaves and pink flowers in early summer. Grows to about 6 feet.

Pernettya mucronata
Above: An evergreen grown mainly for its berries on female plants: shades of red, pink, purple or white according to variety.

Pieris
Above: There are many good species and varieties, grown for their white flowers and red-flushed young leaves. About 6 feet.

Rhododendrons
Above: There are rhododendrons to suit all sizes of garden, and catalogs and garden centers offer hundreds of them.

Skimmia
Glossy-leaved evergreens, with red berries (if you buy a female variety or one that has flowers of both sexes). About 3 feet.

Ground-cover Plants

Ground-cover plants will help to suppress weeds, and if used over a large area will add a sense of texture to the garden floor. Remember, however, that until they become well established, ground-cover plants are as vulnerable to dry soil and competition as most other plants.

SHRUBS

Cotoneaster dammeri
Ground-hugging shrub to about 6 inces. The stems root as they spread to about 3 feet. Red berries in fall.

Erica carnea (spring heath)
Above: Most varieties make a mound of growth about 1 foot high, covered with pink, red or white flowers in winter and spring.

Euonymus fortunei (wintercreeper)
A tough evergreen about 12–18 inches tall with a spread of 2 feet or more. Grow the bright variegated varieties.

Hedera (ivy)
Above: Both small-leafed and large-leafed types of ivy can be used for ground cover.

Hypericum calycinum
(Aaron's beard)
Above: A semi-evergreen about 1 foot tall, with large, yellow flowers and a prominent boss of stamens. A rampant spreader.

Juniperus horizontalis
(creeping juniper)
A ground-hugging conifer with a spread of 4 feet or more. There are several good varieties varying mainly in foliage color.

Lonicera pileata
An evergreen with horizontally spreading branches and small, bright green leaves. Grows to about 2 feet by 4 feet.

Pachysandra terminalis
Above: A low-growing ground cover about 1 foot tall, with white inconspicuous flowers. "Variegata" is a more attractive plant.

Polygonum affine (Himalayan fleece-flower)
Above: Forms a creeping mat of bright green foliage to about 6 inches, with small, pink flowers.

Rosa (rose)
Above: Modern ground-cover roses are very compact and ideal where you need summer color for a sunny site.

Thymus serpyllum
(mother-of-thyme)
Above: Ground-hugging plant with aromatic foliage and clusters of, purple, white, pink or red flowers.

Vinca (periwinkle)
Above: A rather untidy, spreading ground cover, but useful for its usually blue flowers all summer long. There are also variegated forms.

BORDER PERENNIALS

Acaena (sheepburr)
Above: A colonizing carpeter with small, fern-like leaves, to about 2-3 inches high. Brownish-red burrs follow summer flowers.

Ajuga reptans (bugleweed)
Grown primarily for foliage effect. There are purple and variegated varieties that form a carpet 2-4 inches high.

Bergenia
Above: Large, rounded, glossy green, leathery leaves. Flowers – mostly pink – in spring. 1–1½ feet.

Cotula squalida (New Zealand brass-buttons)
An evergreen carpeter with fern-like foliage, growing to about 2 inches. Small yellow flowers.

Epimedium
There are various species, grown mainly for foliage effect. Pale green leaves sometimes flushed brown or bronze. About 9 inches.

Geranium endressii (endres cranesbill)
Above: Deeply lobed foliage topped with pale pink flowers in summer. Dies down in winter.

Hosta
Above: These popular foliage plants come in many variations, so choose species or varieties with leaves that particularly appeal to you.

Lamium maculatum (spotted dead nettle)
A loose carpeter about 9 inches tall. Choose a variety with silvery or attractively mottled foliage.

Lysimachia nummularia (creeping Jenny)
Top: Small, rounded leaves, yellow in "Aurea," and yellow flowers. Needs moist soil, and only retains leaves in winter in mild areas.

Pulmonaria (lungwort)
There are many species and varieties, often with silver-splashed leaves. The spring flowers are in shades of blue and pink.

Stachys byzantina (lamb's-ear)
Above: A gray evergreen with narrow, woolly leaves. Foliage height about 6 inches but purple flower spikes grow to 18 inches.

Tiarella cordifolia (Allegheny foamflower)
Above: A carpeter about 4 inches tall with lobed, hairy leaves, topped with small spikes of white flowers.

Waldsteinia ternata
Above: Evergreen about 4 inches tall, spreading rapidly by creeping, rooting stems. Yellow flowers in spring and early summer.

Planting for Wildlife

Wildlife will be encouraged into your garden by features such as water, bird tables and nest boxes, and plenty of borders to provide shelter and protection. But if you want to encourage bees, birds and butterflies, you also need shrubs to provide the necessary protection and plants that are rich in nectar or have a plentiful supply of berries or seeds that birds like to eat.

SHRUBS

Buddleia davidii (butterfly-bush)
The flowers attract birds, butterflies, bees and many other insects.

Cotoneaster species
Above: The flowers attract insects, the berries bring the birds.

Ilex (holly)
Above: Holly berries are very attractive to birds, but be sure to plant a female variety – otherwise you will not have any berries.

Lavandula (lavender)
Useful for attracting butterflies.

Leycesteria (Himalaya honeysuckle)
Above: Birds love the juicy berries.

Pyracantha (firethorn)
Above: Bees and other insects are attracted to the flowers, and birds eat the berries that follow.

BORDER PLANTS

Aster (Michaelmas daisy)
Above: Butterflies, bees and other insects.

Aubretia
Above: Butterflies, bees and other insects.

Centranthus (Jupiter's beard)
Attracts a wide range of insects.

Erigeron (fleabane)
Butterflies, bees and other insects.

Helenium (sneezeweed)
Butterflies, bees and other insects.

Scabiosa (scabious)
Butterflies, bees and other insects.

Sedum spectabile (showy sedum)
Above: Butterflies, bees and other insects.

Solidago (goldenrod)
Butterflies and insects.

ANNUALS

Iberis (candytuft)
Above: Butterflies and other insects.

Centaurea cyanus (cornflower)
Butterflies and other insects.

Tagetes patula (French marigold)
Above: Butterflies and other insects.

Heliotropium (heliotrope)
Butterflies and other insects.

Reseda (mignonette)
Butterflies and other insects.

Limnanthes douglasii
(meadow-foam)
Above: Butterflies and other insects.

Helianthus (sunflower)
Birds are attracted by the seeds.

Lobularia maritima
(sweet alyssum)
Butterflies and other insects.

Dipsacus (teasel)
Birds are attracted by the seeds.

Cheiranthus (wallflower)
Butterflies and other insects.

Planting for Scent

Scent adds another dimension to the garden, so plant with it in mind. Most people think first of fragrant flowers, but fragrant foliage will remain a feature for a much longer period.

SHRUBS

Chimonanthus praecox
(wintersweet)
Yellow, claw-like flowers in mid- or late winter. Needs a sheltered position and best near the shelter of a wall.

Choisya ternata
(Mexican-orange)
Above: Evergreen, aromatic leaves, yellow in the variety "Sundance." Fragrant white flowers in late spring and into summer.

Cytisus battandieri
(pineapple broom)
Above: Small spikes of yellow flowers in summer, with strong pineapple scent. Requires a sheltered position, perhaps near a wall.

Daphne mezereum
(February daphne)
Dense clusters of highly fragrant, purple-red flowers in late winter and early spring.

Jasminum officinale
(common white jasmine)
A vigorous, twining climber with sweetly scented white flowers, pink in bud, in summer.

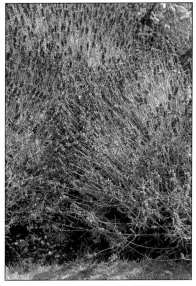

Lavandula (lavender)
Above: Blue, pink or white flowers between midsummer and early fall. Usually gray-green aromatic foliage.

Lonicera fragrantissima (winter honeysuckle)
A twiggy shrub with creamy-white, bell-shaped flowers in mid- and late winter. The scent is strong.

Lonicera periclymenum
(woodbine honeysuckle)
Above: A popular, scented climber. The flowers are a combination of rose-purple and yellow. Early to late summer, depending on variety.

Philadelphus (mock-orange)
Above: There are many good species and varieties, all with white, flowers. Some very fragrant in mid- and late summer.

Rosa (rose)
Above: Roses need no introduction, but the strength of their scent varies, so consult a good catalog if in doubt on this point.

Sarcococca
Clump-forming shrub with glossy, evergreen foliage and white, winter flowers that are small but very fragrant. About 3 feet.

Spartium junceum (Spanish broom)
Almost leafless, rush-like stems with pea-shaped, golden yellow flowers all summer. Sweet honey scent.

Syringa (lilac)
S. vulgaris (common lilac) and other species of these popular and fragrant shrubs, blooming in late spring and early summer.

Viburnum x *bodnantense*
A winter-flowering shrub with small clusters of fragrant pink flowers on bare stems in winter.

Viburnum carlesii
Top: Sweet-scented white or pink flowers, pink in bud, in spring. Foliage usually has good fall tints before droppingß .

Wisteria sinensis
Above: A very popular, large climber with cascades of sweet-scented mauve to purple-lilac flowers in late spring and early summer.

INDEX

Aaron's beard (*Hypericum calycinum*), 184

Acaena (sheepburr), 185

Acanthus spinosissimus (bear's breech), 178

Acer japonicum 'Aureum', 66

Acer palmatum atropurpureum, 117

Achillea, 108, 109

Achillea filipendulina (fernleaf yarrow), 181

Achillea ptarmica, 111

Acid soil, plants for, 183

Aconite, 106

African lily (*Agapanthus*), 178, 181

Agapanthus (lily-of-the-Nile), 178, 181

Agrostemma githago (corn cockle), 114, 115

Ajuga reptans (bugleweed), 185

Alchemilla mollis (lady's mantle), 34, 114, 117, 124

Alkaline soils, 182

Allegheny foamflower (*Tiarella cordifolia*), 185

Allium giganteum (giant onion), 178

Aloe, 140

Alstroemeria ligtu (Peruvian lilies), 108

Anchusa, 109

Anemone japonica, 111, 180

Anemone x *hybrida* (Japanese anemone), 110

Annual border, 100-101

Annuals, 82, 84

Aquatics, planting, 74

Aquilegia alpinum, 82

Arbor, 65

Arches, 68

Arum italicum pictum, 106

Arundo donax, 179

Aster (Michaelmas daisy), 186

Aster novi-belgii, 110

Astilbe, 104, 180

Astrantia (masterwort), 180

Aubretia, 186

Aucuba japonica (Japanese aucuba), 180

Auricula theatre, 136

Autumn border, 110-111

Autumn hanging basket, 150

Autumn, planting in, 159

Azalea, 183

Baby's-breath (*Gypsophila paniculata*), 182

Bamboos, 64

Barbecue, 12, 71

Barberry, 153

Barrenwort (*Epimedium*), 161, 185

Bear's breech (*Acanthus spinosissimus*), 178

Bedding plants, 84-85

Beds, 89-95

feeding, 171

lawn, in, 46

weeds in, 166

Begonia, 84, 101

Berberis, 117

Bergenia (elephant ears), 153, 180, 185

Big blue lily-turf (*Liriope muscari*), 180

Biological control, 173

Birdbath, 69

Bleeding heart (*Dicentra spectabilis*), 180

Border pinks, 34

Borders, 87-90, 98-125

curved, 21

feeding, 171

weeds in, 166

Boundaries, 58-59

Box, 37

Bricks, 10, 54

Broom (*Cytisus*), 181

Brunnera macrophylla, 180

Buddleia davidii (butterfly-bush), 81, 120

Bugleweed (*Ajuga reptans*), 185

Built-in furniture, 71

Bulbs, 44, 137, 160

Busy Lizzie (*Impatiens*), 84

Buttercup winter hazel (*Corylopsis pauciflora*), 183

Butterflies, attracting, 81

Butterfly-bush (*Buddleia davidii*), 81, 120

Cabbage tree (*Cordyline australis*), 179

Calendulas, 34

Calluna vulgaris (heather), 92, 183

Camellias, 180, 183

Campanula lactiflora, 111

Candles, 76, 77

Candytuft (*Iberis*), 187

Carnation (*Dianthus*), 182

Caryopteris x *clandonensis* (hybrid bluebeard), 181

Caterpillars, 172

Catmint (*Nepeta mussinii*), 181

Ceanothus, 122

Centaurea cyanus (cornflower), 187

Centranthus, 187

Cephalaria gigantea, 111

Ceratostigma plumbaginoides, 149

Chalky soil, plants for, 182

Chamaecyparis, 153

Chamaecyparis lawsonia, 94

Chamaecyparis obtusa, 94

Chamomile lawn, 48

Cheiranthus (wallflower), 187

Cheiranthus cheiri (scented wallflower), 106, 107

Chimney pot clematis, 147

Chimonanthus praecox (wintersweet), 188

Choisya, 161

Choisya ternata (Mexican-orange), 87, 188

Chrysanthemum, 110

Circles, multiple and linking, 11

Circular border, 120-121

Circular theme, 10, 18

Cistus (sun rose), 181

Classic topiary, 154

Clay pavers, 10, 54, 65

Clematis, 62, 123, 147, 182

Climbers, 62

Clover lawn, 48

Color schemes, 25

Colorful cooking pot, 149

Colors, 160

Common white jasmine (*Jasminum officinale*), 188

Compositae, 110

Computer, designing by, 17

Concrete paving blocks, 54

Conifers, 93-95, 112

Containers, 22, 53, 128-131

feeding, 170

herbs in, 39

Convallaria majalis (lily-of-the-valley), 96

Convolvulus mauritanicus, 142

Convolvulus cneorum, 181

Copper boiler, spring display in, 134-135

Cordyline australis (cabbage palm), 179

Corn cockle (*Agrostemma githago*), 114, 115

Cornflower (*Centaurea cyanus*), 187

Cornus alba, 112

Cornus stolonifera, 112

Cortaderia selloana (pampas grass), 179

Corylopsis pauciflora (buttercup winter hazel), 183

Cotinus coggygria (smoke bush), 117

Cotoneaster, 182, 184, 186

Cottage gardens, 10, 34-35

Cotula squalida (New Zealand brass-buttons), 185

Courtyard, secluded, 36-37

Crambe cordifolia, 178

Crassula, 138

Creeping Jenny (*Lysimachia*

nummularia), 185

Creeping juniper (*Juniperus horizontalis*), 184

Crocus, 106, 132, 160

Cupressocyparis leylandii, 112

Cupressus filifera aurea, 153

Curved borders, 29

Cuttings, 48

Cytisus (broom), 181

Cytisus battandieri (pineapple broom), 188

Daboecia cantabrica (Irish heath), 183

Daffodils, miniature, 137

Dahlias, 150

Dame's violet (*Hesperis matronalis*), 107

Daphne mezereum (February daphne), 188

Delphinium, 108, 109

Dendranthema, 111

Design

beginning, 19

computer, using, 17

creating, 18

finishing touches, 20

layout, marking, 21

paper, putting on, 16

pattern, 10

priorities, 12

theme, 10

Diagonal theme, 18

Dianthus (carnation, pinks), 182

Dicentra spectabilis (bleeding heart), 180

Dipsacus (teasel), 187

Disguises, 64-65

Dividing clumps, 161

Dogwood, 112

Doronicum (leopardsbane), 182

Downward slope, 26

Dwarf conifers, 94-95

Echinops ritro (small globe thistle), 181

Electric trimmers, 60, 61

Elephant ears (*Bergenia*), 153, 180, 185

Epimedium (barrenwort), 161, 185

Eranthis hyemalis, 112

Eremurus robustus (giant desert-candle), 179

Erica carnea (spring heath), 92, 112, 113, 184

Erica x *darleyensis*, 112
Erigeron (fleabane), 187
Erysimum hieraciifolium
 (Siberian wallflower),
 106, 107
Euonymus fortunei, 150, 184
Euonymus, silver, 153
Euphorbia (spurge), 146, 180
Evergreen garden, 153

Fatsia japonica (Japan fatsia),
 129, 179, 180
Features, 12, 14
February daphne (*Daphne
 mezereum*), 188
Feeding, 170-171
Fences, 58
Fernleaf yarrow (*Achillea
 filipendulina*), 181
Ferns, 116
Fertilizers, 170
Final plan, 22
Firethorn (*Pyracantha*),
 182, 186
Flares, 76, 77
Fleabane (*Erigeron*), 187
Floodlights, 76
Flowerbeds, irregular
 shapes, 20
Focal point plants, 178-179
Focal points, 11, 68-69
Foliage border, 116-117
Foliage shrubs,
 self-sufficient, 87
Forget-me-not (*Myosotis*), 106
Fountains, wall, 72, 73
Foxglove, 123, 146
Foxtail lily (*Eremurus
 robustus*), 179
French marigold (*Tagetes
 patula*), 187
Furniture, 59, 70-71

Gaillardia hybrids, 101
Galvanized bath garden, 146
Garden furniture, 59, 70-71
Garden illusions, 66-67
Garrya elliptica (silk- tassel)
 179
Gateways, 68
Gaultheria procumbens
 (wintergreen), 183
Gaura lindheimeri, 109
Gazania, 138
Geranium, 114, 140, 142,
 181, 185

Giant desert-candle (*Eremurus
 robustus*), 179
Giverny, 106
Golden rod (*Solidago*), 187
Grass, alternatives to, 48-49
Grasses, 90, 179
Gravel, 22
Gravel beds, 99
Gravel border, making, 99
Gravel gardens, 50
Greenfly, 173
Ground cover, 96, 184-185
Gunnera manicata, 179
Gypsophila paniculata
 (baby's-breath), 182

Habitat, garden as, 161
Halesia carolina (snowdrop
 tree), 183
Hamamelis mollis (witch-
 hazel), 180
Hamamelis x *intermedia*
 (witch- hazel), 112
Heather, 92-93, 112, 113, 151,
 183, 184
 conifers, with, 92, 93
Heather window box, 151
Hedera (ivy), 89, 112, 124, 137,
 184
Hedera colchica, 89
Hedges, 58, 60, 61, 68
Helenium (sneezeweed), 187
Helianthemum nummularium
 (rock rose), 181, 182
Helianthus (sunflowers),
 148, 187
Heliotropium (heliotrope), 187
Helleborus (hellebore), 106,
 180, 182
Helleborus foetidus, 112
Herb garden, 38-39
Herb wheel, 39
Herbaceous border plants,
 102-103
Hesperis matronalis (Dame's
 violet), 107
Himalaya honeysuckle
 (*Leycesteria*), 186
Himalayan fleece-flower
 (*Polygonum affine*), 184
Holly (*Ilex*), 180, 186
Honeysuckle (*Lonicera*), 184,
 188
Hosta (plantain-lily), 104,
 111, 116, 117, 180, 185
House and garden, linking, 12

Hyacinth, 44
Hybrid bluebeard (*Caryopteris
 x clandonensis*), 181
Hypericum calycinum
 (Aaron's beard), 184

Iberis (candytuft), 187
Ilex (holly), 180, 186
Impatiens (Busy Lizzie), 84
Insecticides, 173
Inula, 149
Iris, 106, 122
Iris germanica, 181
Iris pseudacorus, 119
Irish heath (*Daboecia*), 183
Island border, 118, 119
Ivy (*Hedera*), 89, 112,
 124, 137, 184
 golden, 149
 variegated, 150

Japan fatsia (*Fatsia japonica*),
 129, 179, 180
Japanese aucuba (*Aucuba
 japonica*), 180
Japanese anemone (*Anemone* x
 hybrida), 110
Jasminum officinale (common
 white jasmine), 188
Juniperus horizontalis
 (creeping juniper), 184

Kalmia latifolia (mountain-
 laurel), 183
Kitchen garden, 40-41
Knautia macedonica, 114
Kniphofia (red hot poker), 68

L-shaped gardens, 30
Lady's mantle (*Alchemilla
 mollis*), 34, 114, 117, 124
Lamb's-ear (*Stachys
 byzantina*), 185
Lamium, 114
Lamium maculatum
 (spotted dead nettle), 185
Lampranthus, 138
Lantana, 142
Lavender (*Lavandula*), 122,
 182, 186, 188
Lavender cotton (*Santolina
 chamaecyparissus*), 181
Lawn, 44-49
 feeding, 171
 making border in, 98
 moss in, 169

tree in, 88
 weeds, killing, 168,-169
Leaves, raking up, 88
Leopardsbane (*Doronicum*),
 182
Leycesteria (Himalaya
 honeysuckle), 186
Lighting, 76-77
Ligularia dentata, 119
Lilac (*Syringa*), 182
Lilies, 122
Lily-of-the-Nile (*Agapanthus*),
 178, 181
Lily-of-the-valley
 (*Convallaria majalis*), 96
Lilyturf (*Liriope muscari*), 180
Limnanthes douglasii
 (meadow-foam), 187
Liriope muscari (big blue
 lily-turf), 180
Lobelia, 142
Lobelia cardinalis, 119
Lobelia erinus, 101
Lobularia maritima
 (sweet alyssum), 106,
 107, 187
Long, narrow gardens,
 28-29
Lonicera (honeysuckle), 184,
 188
Love-in-a-mist (*Nigella*), 34
Low-voltage lighting, 76
Low walls, 58, 59
Lungwort (*Pulmonaria*), 180,
 185
Lysimachia nummularia
 (creeping Jenny), 185

Mahonia, 179, 180
Making borders, 98-99
Masterwort (*Astrantia*), 180
Matricaria, 101
Mature garden, transforming, 11
Meadow-foam (*Limnanthse
 douglasii*), 187
Mealy bugs, 173
Measuring, 14
Meditation border, 124-125
Mediterranean garden, 140-141
Mesembryanthemum, 138
Mexican-orange (*Choisya
 ternata*), 87, 188
Michaelmas daisies (*Aster*), 186
Mignonette (*Reseda*), 187
Miniature spring garden, 132
Mirrors, 67
Mock-orange (*Philadelphus*),
 188
Moss, 169
Mother-of-thyme (*Thymus
 serpyllum*), 184
Mountain laurel (*Kalmia
 latifolia*), 183
Mowing edge, 98
Mulches, 162-165
Mulching, 98
Mullein (*Verbascum*), 181
Myosotis (forget-me-not), 106

Narrow garden, 32
Nasturtium tropaeolum, 101
Natural stone paving, 37
Nepeta mussinii (catmint), 181
New Zealand brass-buttons
 (*Cotula squalida*), 185

New Zealand flax (*Phormium tenax*), 179
Nigella (love-in-a-mist), 34

Origanum laevigatum, 119
Ornamental vegetables, 41
Osteospermum jucundum, 119
Outdoor rooms, 32-33
Outline, creating, 24
Pachysandra terminalis, 153, 180, 184
Paeonia (peony), 182
Paeonia suffruticosa (tree peony), 182
Pampas grass (*Cortaderia selloana*), 179
Pansies, 150, 152
Papaver, 109
Papaver rhoeas, 114
Paths, 54-55
    weeding, 167
Patio flares, 76, 77
Patios, 52-53
Paulownia tomentosa, 179
Pavers, 54, 55
Paving, 54-57
Pebble pool, 72
Pebble texture, 57
Pebbles, 89
Penstemon, 109
Peony (*Paeonia*), 182
Perennials, 84
    self-sowing, 82
Pergola, 12, 30
Periwinkle (*Vinca*), 134, 180, 184
Pernettya mucronata, 183
Peruvian lily (*Alstroemeria ligtu*), 108
Pests, 172-173
Petunia, 142
Philadelphus (mock-orange), 188
Phormium tenax (New Zealand flax), 179
Picket fences, 58, 59
Pineapple broom (*Cytisus battandieri*), 188
Pieris, 183
Pinks (*Dianthus*), 182
Plantain-lily (*Hosta*), 104, 111, 116, 117, 180, 185
Planning
    final plan, 22
    grids, using, 18
    measuring, 14
    paper, putting plan on, 16
    planting, for, 24-25

scale drawing, 16
shape, 18
surveying, 14
triangulation, 17
using plan, 17
Planting, 159-161
Planting plan, 24-25
Plastic, planting through, 93
Polygonum affine (Himalayan fleece-flower), 184
Ponds, 74-75, 80
Pool, pebble, 72
Populus serotina, 118
Potager, 40
Potentilla, 104
Potting-on, 158
Primroses, 132
    auricula, 136
Pruning, 86
    chemical, 60
Prunus x *subhirtella*, 113
Pulmonaria (lungwort), 180, 185
Pyracantha (firethorn), 182, 186

Raised beds, 33
Rectangular theme, 10, 18
Red hot poker (*Kniphofia*), 68
Red spider mite, 173
Renovating border, 99
Repotting, 158
Reseda (mignonette), 187
Reticulata iris, 132
Rhododendron, 180, 183
Rock gardens, 27
Rock rose (*Helianthemum nummularium*), 181, 182
Romantic border, 122-123
Rose border, 114-115
Rosemary, prostrate, 140
Roses, 62, 122, 123, 184, 188
    border, in, 161
Rubus biflorus, 112
Rubus cockburnianus, 112
Rudbeckia, 111

Salvia guaranitica, 119
Salvia turkestanica, 109
Salvia uliginosa, 109
Sambucus nigra, 118
Santolina chamaecyparissus (lavender cotton), 181
Sarcococca (sweet box), 180, 188

Scabiosa (scabious), 182, 187
Scale insects, 172
Scent, planting for, 188
Scented wallflower (*Cheiranthus cheiri*), 106, 107
Schizachyrium scoparium, 113
Screens, 64-65
Seaside garden, 138
Sedum spectabile (showy sedum), 110, 111, 187
Sedum spurium, 85
Seeds, sowing, 158
Self-sowing, 82
Senecio, 181
Shady gardens, plants for, 180
Shape, planning, 18
Sheepburr (*Acaena*), 185
Showy sedum (*Sedum spectabile*), 187
Shrubs, 86-87, 161
Siberian wallflower (*Erysimum hieraciifolium*), 106, 107
Silk-tassel (*Garrya elliptica*), 179
Sisyrinchium striatum, 122, 123
Skimmia, 180, 183
Slopes, 14, 15, 26-27
Slugs, 172
Small globe thistle (*Echinops ritro*), 181
Smoke bush (*Cotinus coggygria*), 117
Snails, 172
Sneezeweed (*Helenium*), 187
Snowdrop tree (*Halesia carolina*), 183
Solanum jasminoides, 122
Solidago (golden rod), 187
Spanish broom (*Spartium junceum*), 188
Spotlights, 76, 77
Spotted dead nettle (*Lamium maculatum*), 185
Spring border, 106-107
Spring garden, miniature, 132
Spring heath (*Erica carnea*), 92, 112, 113, 184
Spring, planting in, 159
Spurge (*Euphorbia*), 180

Stachys byzantina (lamb's-ear), 185
Statues, 68, 69
Strawberries, Alpine, 144
Summer border, 108-109
Summer flower basket, 142-143
Summerhouse, 30
Sundial, 68, 69
Sunflower (*Helianthus*), 148, 187
    seed, from, 158
Sunny and dry areas, plants for, 181
Sun rose (*Cistus*), 181
Surveying, 14
Sweet alyssum (*Lobularia maritima*), 106, 107, 187

Tagetes patula (French marigold), 187
Taxus baccata (yew), 124
Teasel (*Dipsacus*), 187
Terracing, 26
Terracotta planter of spring bulbs, 137
Terracotta pots, 132
Thalictrum aquilegiifolium, 114
Thuja plicata, 124
Thyme, golden, 140
Thyme lawn, 48-49
Thymus serpyllum (mother-of-thyme), 184
Tiarella cordifolia (Allegheny foamflower), 185
Tool shed, 12
Trachycarpus fortunei (windmill palm), 179
Tree peony (*Paeonia suffruticosa*), 182
Tree seats, 70, 71
Trees, 88-89
Trellis, painted, 64
Triangulation, 17
Trompe l'oeil, 66-67
Trug of winter pansies, 152
Tub, planting, 130
Tulip, 122, 134, 137

Upward slope, 27
Urn, planting, 130

Vegetables, 40-41
Verbascum, 108, 109, 181, 182
Viburnum carlesii, 188

Viburnum davidii, 180
Viburnum x *bodnantense*, 113, 188
Vinca (periwinkle), 134, 180, 184
Vine weevils, 172
Viola cornuta, 124
Violet, 134, 146

Waldsteinia ternata, 185
Wall fountains, 72, 73
Wallflower (*Cheiranthus*), 187
Water, 72-74
Watering, 174-177
Weedkillers, using, 167
Weeds, 166-169
    ground cover suppressing, 96
Whitefly, 172
Wild flowers, 80
Wild strawberry basket, 144
Wild-flower lawn, 45
Wildlife garden, 45, 80-81
Wildlife, planting for, 186-187
Windmill palm (*Trachycarpus fortunei*), 179
Window box, heather, 151
Winter border, 112-113
Winter green (*Gaultheria procumbens*), 183
Wintersweet (*Chimonanthus praecox*), 188
Wisteria sinensis, 188
Witch-hazel (*Hamamelis*), 112, 180

Yarrow (*Achillea filipendulina*), 181
Yew (*Taxus baccata*), 124
Yucca, 181
Yucca filamentosa, 179
Yucca gloriosa, 179

ACKNOWLEDGMENTS

All special photography by John Freeman.

The publishers would like to thank the following picture libraries
for allowing reproduction of their photographs:

Key: t=top; b=bottom; l=left; c=center; r=right.

Garden Picture Library: pages 112 (*Howard Rice*); 113
(*Brigitte Thomas*).
Jerry Harpur Garden Picture Library: pages 2tr, tl; 11bl; 12br; 32;
33; 34; 37; 55; 64; 65; 67r; 70t; 73tl; 77l, br; 81l; 101; 106; 114;
116; 129; 131l.
Peter McHoy: pages 1; 7; 10; 11tl; 12t; 13; 15; 22; 23; 27; 39br;
44tr, br; 45tr; 47; 54; 57; 60; 61; 62b; 63; 66tl bl; 68; 69; 71; 73tr,
bl; 74; 78; 80; 81tr; 83; 85; 87; 89; 91; 93t; 97; 99; 103; 104bl, tr;
105; 128; 129tr; 157; 161; 163t; 172; 173l; 175; 176t; 178; 179;
180; 181; 182; 183; 184; 185; 186; 187; 188.
Derek St. Romaine: pages 111; 115; 117; 119; 122; 123; 124.
David Way: pages 107; 120; 121; 125t.

The publishers would also like to thank the following owners for
permission to include their gardens in the book:

Drs. and Mevr. F.J. Arnold, Wijchen, The Netherlands; Mrs Natalie
Finch, Colchester, Essex; RHS Wisley, Surrey; Mr Ernie Taylor,
Great Barr, Birmingham; Mrs Maureen Thompson, Long Melford,
Suffolk; Lady Tollemache, Helmingham Hall, Stowmarket, Suffolk;
Mr David Way, Southover, Maidstone, Kent.

Finally, the publishers would like to acknowledge the invaluable
help of the following:

Andy Sturgeon at The Fitted Garden, Garson Farm Garden
Centre, Winterdown Road, West End, Esher, Surrey, KT10 8LS, for
producing some of the practical sequences for photography;
Country World, Crews Hill, Enfield, for providing locations for
step photography; Chelsea Gardener, 125 Sydney Street, London
SW3, for providing containers for the *Container Gardening*
section; and Brenda Hyatt, 1, Toddington Crescent, Blue Bell Hill,
Chatham, Kent, for providing the auriculas on page 136.

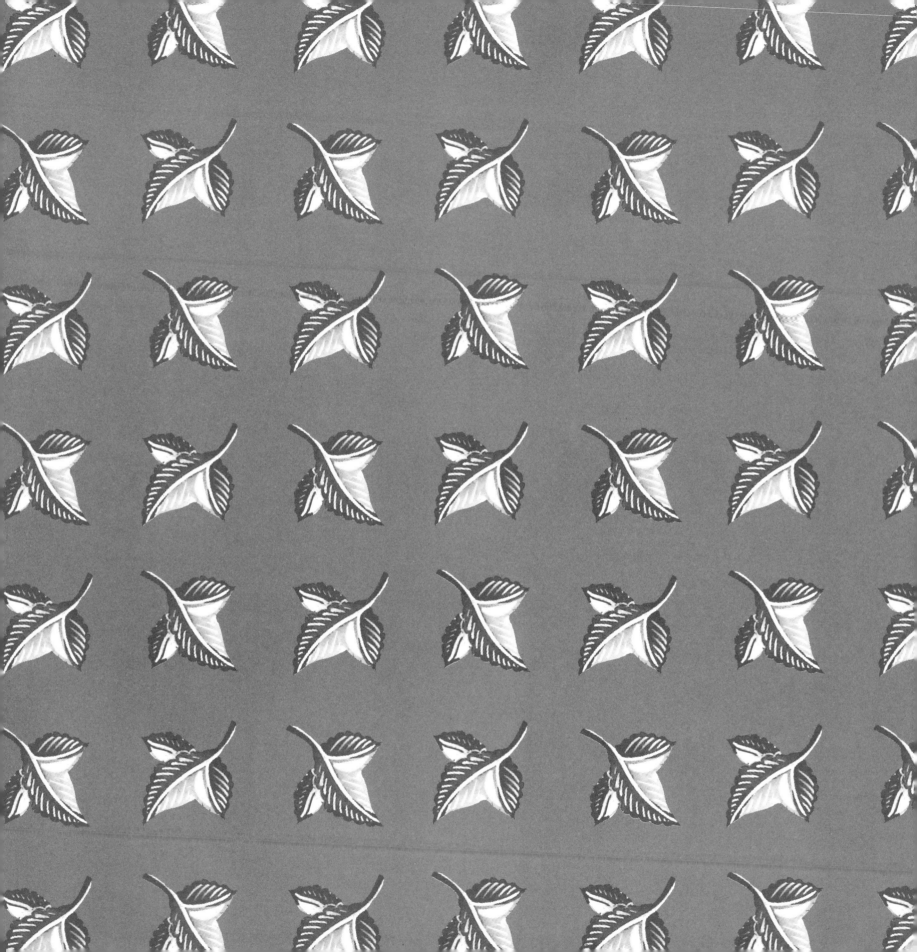